DJABUGAY COUNTRY

DJABUGAY COUNTRY

An Aboriginal History of Tropical North Queensland

TIMOTHY BOTTOMS

ALLEN & UNWIN

First published in 1999 by
Allen & Unwin
83 Alexander Street, Crows Nest NSW 2065, Australia
Phone: (61 2) 8425 0100
Fax: (61 2) 9906 2218
E-mail: frontdesk@allen-unwin.com.au
Web: http://www.allenandunwin.com

National Library of Australia
Cataloguing-in-Publication entry:

Bottoms, Timothy (Timothy David Reis).
    Djabugay country: an aboriginal history of tropical North Queensland.

    Bibliography.
    Includes index.
    ISBN 1 86508 031 4.

    1. Djabugay (Australian people)—History. 2. Aborigines, Australian—Queensland—Cairns Region—History. 3. Cairns Region (Qld.)—Race relations—History. I. Title

994.360049915

Set in 11/13pt Bembo by DOCUPRO, Sydney
Printed by Brown Prior Anderson Pty Ltd, Burwood, Victoria

10 9 8 7 6 5 4 3 2

Djabugay

Foreword

This book introduces our people to the whole of Australia, and how we as Aboriginals experienced and remembered those early days. Governments with their policies of the times did not realise how much suffering was put upon Aboriginal people and we hope the reader will gain an insight into what really happened and appreciate our story. It is sad but true that although we gained the right to vote, drive cars, travel and attend hotels, we are in many ways no better off. Successive governments, their institutions and values still dictate and dominate our situation. So much of our culture and land still remains stolen, and our views ignored. We wonder, what does it take to acknowledge the truth of our history, and the impact it has had on us? We trust and believe in a better future for our people, and hope that *Djabugay Country* will assist Australians everywhere to understand and accept the truths of the past and step with us towards Reconciliation and an honest future for all our children.

Selwyn Hunter

Florence Williams

Enid Boyle

Esther Snider

Wilfred Levers

Elaine Chookie

Steven Fagan

Mona Fagan

Milton Brim

Lyn Hobbler

Marita Hobbler

Winnie Brim

Djabugay Elders

Djabugay

Preface

In the lead-up to the new millennium, Australians are caught in an identity crisis concerning the position of the indigenous peoples of the nation. Land rights, our colonial story and the desire for reconciliation are hot buttons in the national psyche.

A prerequisite to reconciliation has to be acknowledgement of the truths of the past. More often than not, these truths are not pretty. The colonial story left the country with what the Governor General, Sir William Deane, described together with his then colleague on the High Court of Australia, Justice Mary Gaudron, as a 'legacy of unutterable shame'.

For the New Australians these are bracing truths. The triumphalist view of the past—based solely on pride in achievement and frontier bravery and perseverance—must now contend with stories of frontier cowardice and inhumanity that challenge the former perspective. These truths are uncomfortable for Australians who have for too long been fed on jingoistic histories. The new histories which have emerged over the past three decades have revealed a complex and troubling past.

These histories are not only bracing for the nation as a whole, they are bracing for local communities and regions because they tell the story of familiar landscapes, place names, sites and landmarks.

These are places where acts of gross cruelty and heartlessness took place; where blood and tears were spilt.

For North Queenslanders, Timothy Bottoms' *Djabugay Country* reveals a jarring new view of a familiar landscape, which will be alien to most North Queenslanders: the swimming holes where children now play were once places of great misery; at Crystal Cascades a mother and child fled for their lives from the massacre of their people at Speewah; the silence of Black Mountain was once shattered by the cries of dying humans when Molloy 'taught the blacks a lesson' for stealing his draft horses. Supermarkets and canefields now sprawl over the sacred places, the byways, homes and meeting places of the Djabugay.

Remember the immense tragedy wrought by psychopathic retribution at Port Arthur in 1996? And the way this tore into the lives of families, communities and the nation? The Djabugay suffered likewise and were left destitute following the destruction of their economy and the desecration of their religious places.

Timothy Bottoms joins fellow North Queensland historians Henry Reynolds, Dawn May and Noel Loos, who have each made such a great contribution to illuminating the truths of our frontier past.

Good history is the pursuit of truth. Reconciliation is, above all, a test of maturity. For Australians generally, and the people of North Queensland particularly, it will mean coming to terms with the past that Timothy Bottoms is describing here.

Noel Pearson
Cairns
November 1998

Djabugay

Acknowledgements

I am indebted to the Elders for their trust in me, as well as for sharing so much of their oral history. Similarly, the guidance and advice from *Bina*, Michael Quinn, for Chapter 1 was immeasurable, as was that of Ross Verevis for contemporary material in Chapter 4. I am grateful to Bruce Breslin for his unstinting editorial comment and Nick Heijm for his astute insights; Rob Hinxman for his thoughtful observations; Kathy Frankland and Margaret Reid from the Office of Family and Personal Histories, at the Queensland State Archives; and Brian Townend of The Seventh Day Adventist Archives at The Library, Avondale College, Cooranbong, NSW for his assistance.

The role the members of the Djabugay History Reference Group—Rhonda Brim, Barry Hunter Snr and Rosetta Brim—played in the process was most helpful. I thank the Jilli Binna Museum and Les Sim of the Historical Society of Cairns, as well as the John Oxley Library and the Australian Institute for Aboriginal and Torres Strait Islander Studies, for their assistance with the photographs. Thanks also to Kaeleen Hunter and Carol Estree for photographs, and Mrs Esme Hudson for sharing her Exemption Papers and her kind hospitality.

Terry Straight and MultiVisuals and the Tjapukai Cultural Park gave permission to use the photograph of Walter Brim and Bertie

Riley for the front cover. My grateful appreciation goes to Michael Watt for his generous assistance in taking contemporary photographs, and to Steve Lane for his generosity in preparing the maps.

This project was developed with the financial support of the Community and Personal Histories Grants Program of the Queensland Department of Families, Youth and Community Care and the Queensland Community History (Indigenous Heritage) Grants Program of the Department of Environment. Our grateful appreciation to the Queensland Department of Families, Youth and Community Care for the publishing grant which helped bring this work to fruition. Finally, I wish to express my sincere thanks to the Mantaka 'Shanty' Aboriginal Corporation for their faith in me for the project and their support and sponsorship.

Contents

Djabugay

Maps

Djabugay

Illustrations

Djabugay

A Guide to Djabugay Pronunciation

VOWEL SOUNDS

For simplicity the linguistic approach of using [:] to indicate a lengthened vowel sound, such as [a:], [i:], or [u:] has been ignored and the doubling of the letter has been adopted. For example, [a:] is pronounced as [aa], [i:] as [ii], and [u:] as [uu].

[a] is pronounced like the vowel in come, some.

[i] is pronounced like the vowel in lit, bit, bin.

[u] is pronounced like the vowel in look, took or book.

CONSONANTS

[b], [d], [l], [m], [n], [w] and [y] are pronounced as in English.

[g] is pronounced as in gas, gun or gate.

[r] is pronounced as in part.

[rr] is rolled like the Scottish 'r'.

[dj] is pronounced as a 'd' and a 'j' at the same time, but sharper, as in the 'j' sound in judge or jury.

[ay] like 'eye'—in Djabugay, Gunggay.

[ng] like ringer, if you omit the first and last two letters.

Please note: For a more precise approach, reference should be made to M. Quinn and R. Banning's work, in particular, *Djabugay Ngirrma Gulu*, Cairns, 1989, pp. 110–11.

Djabugay

Glossary

Bama rainforest Aboriginal people/person.

bayu hut (beehive shaped).

Budaadji carpet snake, associated with (or in another form of the) rainbow serpent.

Bulmba habitable place/country.

Bulurru Religion/Law/Storywater.

Burrawungal/Bunanda female water sprite.

Burri-Burri older initiated men.

Damarri heroic *Bulurru*/Storywater character, an opposite to his brother *Guyala*.

djimburru walking tracks.

djimurru large hut for 30 or 40 people.

Gadja 'spirit of a dead person' usually male, referring to Europeans.

Gudju-Gudju Bulurru/Storytime rainbow serpent (and also a rainbow).

Gurrabana Wet Season; moietal classification.

Gurra-Gurra ancestors.

Gurraminya Dry Season; moietal classification.

Guyala heroic *Bulurru*/Storywater character, an opposite to his brother *Damarri*.

maa (or *mayi*) edible plant food.

maladambun sorcerer.

minya edible meat.

warrma dance/corroboree.

wayan 'clever-men', 'men of high degree' or 'medicine men'.

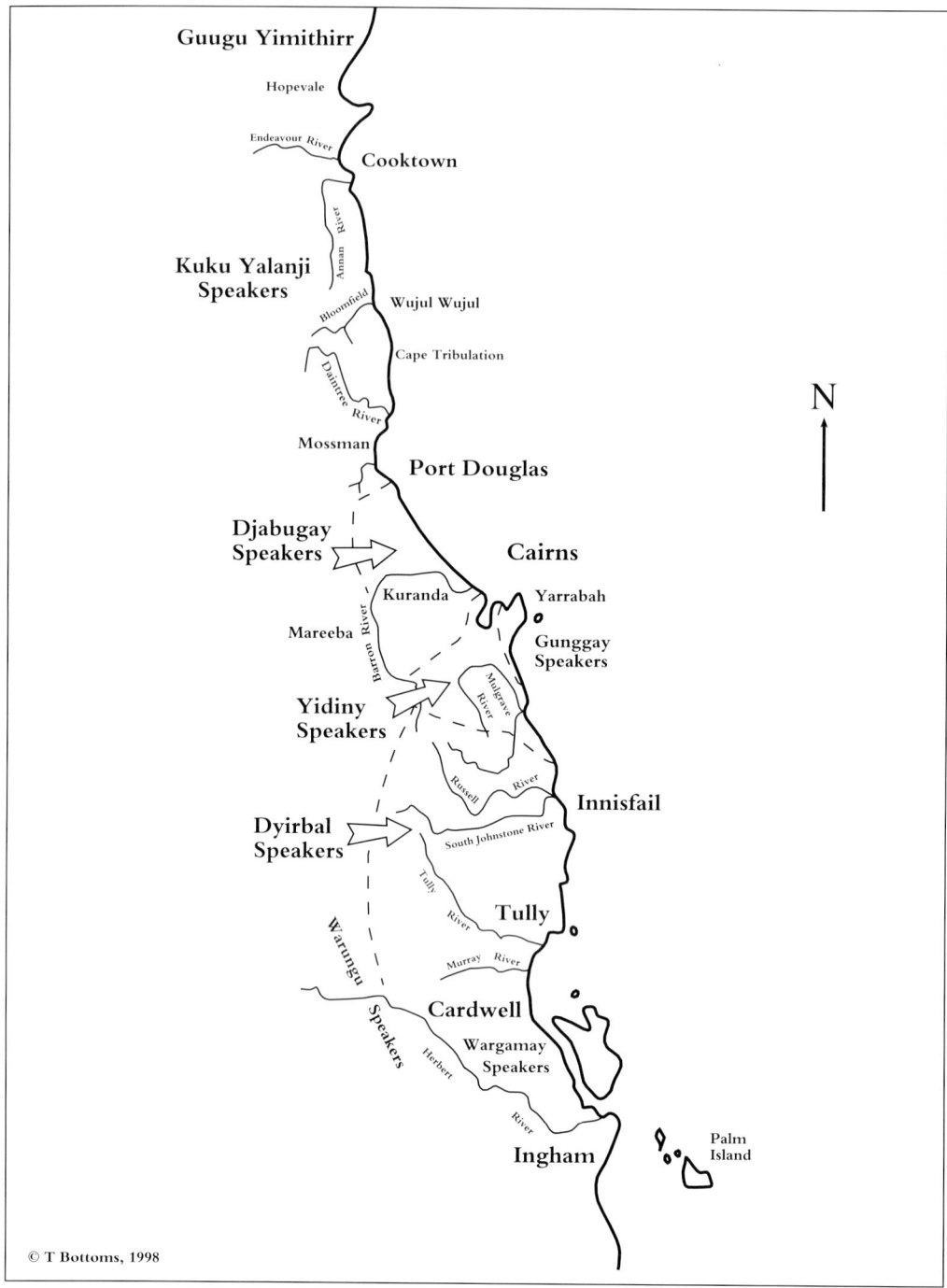

Map 1 *A guide to tribal locations in the rainforests of Far North Queensland*

Djabugay

1
Journeys of the Gurra-Gurra (Ancestors)

Since time immemorial, Aboriginal Australia has flourished across the largest island continent in the world. Over 700 nations/ tribes,[1] speaking more than 250 languages,[2] have occupied the entire continent for untold millennia.

From the coastal groups to the savanna and desert peoples to those occupying the mountainous regions and colder climes that bespeak the south-eastern corner of the Australian continent, all these many and varied indigenous Australians utilised the environment peculiar to their area, not only to be nourished by the spirituality that was imprinted on the land, but also to gain physical sustenance. While each Aboriginal environment may have varied, the spiritual and religious views of their world were relatively homogenous. There is a commonality in religious beliefs across Australia. The Dreaming and the Dreaming Place beliefs of central Australia have their analogues here in Far North Queensland, in beliefs in *Bulurru*, translated as Storytime (the time of the world's making). This refers to the time of creation, and of the events and beings of that time, who are ever-present in the land, in its Storyplaces and Storywaters.

The unique rainforest environment of Far North Queensland is the home of the Djabuganydji, one of the many groups of rainforest people. They spoke Djabugay (or 'Tjapukai'), whilst other rainforest Bama between Ingham and Cooktown spoke dialects of the five major languages of the region (see Map 1).[3] ('Tjapukai' is the spelling devised by Dr N. B. Tindale in 1938, and is now used in reference to the Tjapukai Aboriginal Cultural Park. 'Djabugay' is the current linguistic spelling and is considered the appropriate way of referring to the people.)

Archaeological evidence confirms that Aborigines have occupied the Cairns rainforest region for at least 5100 years,[4] with carbon dating for Mt Mulligan (west of Mareeba) recording an occupancy of 37 500 years.[5] Pollen deposits found at Lynchs Crater on the Atherton Tablelands suggest that occupation in that area dates from 45 000 years.[6] Drill core samples from the Great Barrier Reef, eighty kilometres east of Cairns, suggest 'Australia was inhabited 140 000 years ago'.[7] Ursula McConnel reported that 'when the coral reef was all scrubland' the Djabuganydji used to go out as far as the Barrier Reef, which suggests that, as the sea levels were lower then, their hunting grounds extended out that far. McConnel also reported that an ancestor spirit, the blue-tongued lizard, broke some taboo and caused the flood.[8] Whatever the scientists may conclude, one cannot doubt that indigenous Australians have been here 'since time immemorial'.

In the same fashion as other indigenous people throughout the world, the Bama perceived the landscape as embodying their spiritual heritage.

> Creation stories from the Dreaming are important links between indigenous Australians and their traditional country, often explaining how features of the landscape were formed while also affirming important community values and customary laws.[9]

In this regard, the Djabuganydji, who now refer to themselves as Djabugay, and whose homelands are to the north and west of modern Cairns, are no exception. The tribal groupings that speak dialects of Djabugay are the Djabuganydji (Jabu-ganji), the Nyagali (Na-kali), the Guluy (Koo-lie), the Buluwanydji (Bull-a-wan-ji),[10] and on the coastal strip, the Yirrganydji (Ira-kan-ji).[11] The southern half of the Cairns rainforest region is home to the linguistically related Yidiny-speakers.[12] These people not only shared a similar social organisation but also a Story-Law heritage. The Djabugay and their neighbours, the Yidinydji and Gungganydji, also shared a similar pattern of social organisation. The societies were divided into moieties (two parts): the Wet Season side (*Gurrabana*) and the Dry Season side (*Gurraminya*).[13] Each side was made up of clans and these had their own individual totems, as well as sharing moiety totems. The marriage laws enforced marriage between the moieties, it being forbidden to have sexual relations within one's own moiety.

The religious beliefs of the Djabugay and their neighbours pervaded every aspect of life. The landscape itself is informed by the Storied Past. Features of the landscape have their place in the Creation Stories, and these Stories link each Bama group to their *Bulmba* (habitable place/homeland). It is this Storied Past which tells of the activities of the *Gurra-Gurra* or ancestors. Mirroring the actions of the *Gurra-Gurra*, the way of life is clearly outlined. Continuing in this 'way', the Bama have walked in confidence, secure in the knowledge that others have so walked in safety before them.[14]

> These Stories speak the country, revealing it to be not a wilderness, but a humanised world, partaking of the spirit of the ancestors, their blood, their bones, their story, ever-present in the land and in its creatures. Just as a map serves to orient its reader, these Stories in celebrating the topography serve as an aid to orientation, not just the lie of the land, but as to its socially derived meaning and significance. Yet the land is more than symbolic, does not merely point to something beyond itself . . . it is that Other.
>
> That's the waters talking . . . **Bulurru**.[15]

It is as the late Djabugay Elder, Nyuwarri stated:

Bulurru, that's the Spirit in the water
Gudju Gudju, the Rainbow.
When you see that Rainbow
wonderful he shows.
That's Our Father.[16]

The voice of *Gudju-Gudju* is heard in the thunder and is a sign that the spirit of the Law is angry with people and is seeking out wrong-doers. Belief in *Gudju-Gudju* was central to indigenous healing and the initiation of *wayan*—'clever-men', 'men of high degree' or 'medicine men'.[17] There was also the *Maladambun* (sorcerer) in Djabugay society. He could have a profound influence in the community with many people going lame or dying as a consequence of his powers. The *wayan* was often called upon to heal the sick and take off the 'magic'.[18] For the Djabugay and their neighbours, the Yidinydji and Gungganydji, *Gudju-Gudju* was an important wet-side (*Gurrabana*) totem. In fact, all over Australia, beliefs in the rainbow

1.1 Wangal Djungay, *meaning place where the fast-moving Storytime boomerang landed, known today as Double Island. It is also associated with* Gudju-Gudju *(the Rainbow Serpent) and is linked to the* Mira Warrigala *Gungganydji of King Beach, Cape Grafton (opposite* Gububarra—Fitzroy Island). Yilamaga, *the place of healing waters is an important Bulurru Storywater site and is perceived to be the mouth of* Gudju-Gudju. *It also has an important association for the Yidinydji, to the west.*

(Photo courtesy of Michael Watt.)

serpent are prevalent, and so possibly these beliefs represent an older strata of indigenous religious thought. It is suggested that Djabuganydji and Gungganydji met on *Wangal Djungay* (Double Island)—the home of *Gudju-Gudju*—to perform *warrma* (dance/corroboree) in his honour.[19]

Throughout Australia the rainbow snake is associated with many river courses, and here *Gudju-Gudju* in the guise of *Budaadji*, the carpet snake, is said to have made the rivers and creeks from Crystal Cascades to Kuranda. To the northern Djabugay, whose traditional lands include the valley of the Mowbray River, *Budaadji*

originated around Kuranda, . . . close by Black Mountain to the Mowbray River, which it follows to the mouth. Here he travels under the surface to a swamp near the mangroves around the south end of Four Mile Beach, then passes along the beach area to the hill at Port Douglas itself, where he again goes underground and remains to the present.[20]

(To the Kuku Yalanji, who shared resources with the Djabugay at Island Point, *Budaadji* equates with *Kurriyala*.)

One Story has it that *Gudju-Gudju* rose from the sea, covered in *miya-miya* (nautilus shells). In the form of *Budaadji*, he made his way up the Barron Gorge to give the shells to the people of the Tablelands in exchange for *yimbi* (dilly-bags). He returned to the sea, promising to bring back more shells. On a trip back up to the Tablelands, he was ambushed by greedy bird-men who wanted the shells. They cut him up and took the shells for themselves.[21] The Story appears to

1.2 Burri-burri *(fully initiated man) making a* Djigarra Yimbi *(half-moon or bicornual basket) from* bugul *(Calamus caryotoides—split lawyer cane). This style of basket is unique to the rainforest Bama and is strong and durable. Both men and women used them, as it was designed to hang from the forehead down the back, allowing the owner's hands to be free to perform other tasks. (R. Duffin & R. Brim, Ngapi* Garrang Bulurru-m, All things Come from Bulurru, Jilli Binna, *Cairns, 1992, p. 9.)*

(Photo courtesy of John Oxley Library.)

relate to the trading practices of coastal and Tableland people. Walter Roth recorded that, 'For the purposes of trade and barter . . . the Barron River Natives wander[ed] up the coast as far as Port Douglas and inland up to Kuranda and Mareeba' where 'square-cut nautilus shell necklaces' and 'hour-glass woven dilly-bags and round-based basket dilly-bags' were a part of the trading items.[22]

In another account of the *Budaadji* Story, *Budaadji* is a man carrying shells up the Barron River to the Tablelands. He carted shells from the north, which suggests Port Douglas way. According to Roth 'square nautilus cut necklaces were trade items from Pt. Douglas in the north'.[23] On his journey he stopped at *Bubundji* (place of the she-oak trees), the camp at the confluence of Freshwater Creek and coastal Barron River. He 'sat down to hear the waters sing',[24] possibly at *Diiwunga*, Stoney Creek Falls. Stoney Creek is known as *Garndal-Garndal*. Other places mentioned on his journey are *Waalara* (Surprise Creek) and *Mayula* (Robb's Monument). In this account he is also cut up by greedy bird-men, and the pieces of his body thrown into the bush. P. C. Griffin recorded that, amongst the Gungganydji, 'the water which is near the story-stone at Bucki and which we see start up on the side of Kaligraba or Grant Hill, really comes down from the tableland, for the tail of Kutcha-Kutcha is up there and the head of him is down here'.[25] This would suggest that *Gudju-Gudju*'s body landed far and wide in the realm of the Djabugay/Yidiny-speaking Bama, and therefore links these people to a shared Storywater.[26] The Story of *Budaadji* appears to be written across the body of the land.

Other figures from the Storytime of primary significance to the Djabugay and their neighbours are the brothers *Damarri* and *Guyala*, who are credited with setting in place the marriage laws and system of social organisation.[27] These two brothers are said to have come from the north. The Story says they were taller than the local people and skilled in the art of fighting. The people of the rainforest were of a small stature. They are credited with giving the people the knowledge of how to get poison out of toxic foods.

It might be that *Damarri* and *Guyala* were actually real men, passing on vital knowledge. They are ascribed with teaching the people how to make fire and traps for animals. However, the Stories give them magical creative powers. The brothers were always arguing about the way life should be difficult or easy, and, more often than not, *Damarri* got his way. Life was shaped by their arguments, so that, for instance, certain foods became toxic and required much treatment.[28] Fortunately *Guyala* had his way over naming of places. *Damarri* wanted to name only a few places on a journey; but *Guyala* thought it would be easier for people to follow a route if many places were named. They are said to have put different foods in their place in the natural environment and to have created features of the landscape.[29] *Damarri* is said to have stemmed the sea level by getting his off-siders to build many fires along the coast and put *bayngga* (hot rocks) along the water's edge.[30] Geologists have confirmed that the sea level along the Cairns coastline has risen over the past 15 000 years and reached its present level around 6000 BP.[31]

In *Damarri*'s endeavours to make life more difficult for people, one Story has it that he gave *ganyarra* (the crocodile) its teeth and lost a leg in the process.[32] And once, angered by his brother who had asked him to make fire, he made rock and fire come out of the ground, creating *Bunda Djarrugan* (Scrub Hen Mountain—Walsh's Pyramid).[33] It could be that the exploits of these two brothers have been enhanced over time and 'god-like' powers attributed to them. The Gungganydji believe that *Damarri* lies protecting what is now Yarrabah and the traditional lands of the Gungganydji.[34] One of Griffin's sources said that *Damarri* is present in the Freshwater Creek area, as an impression in the ground.[35]

Glacier Rock[36] and around to North Peak[37] are also associated

1.3 *Glacier Rock (centre) around (to the left) to North Peak (out of sight) are associated with* Damarri's *resting place. Smith's track ran up the range on the left, while Douglas' track came down the range immediately to the right of Glacier Rock. The Barron Gorge, through which flows* Bana Bidagarra *(coastal Barron River), is located over the small range seen on the right. Lake Placid is to be found at the foot of the range in the centre.*

(Photo courtesy of Michael Watt.)

1.4 *To the Redlynch Djabugay in the Freshwater Valley,* Damarri *is lying face down; head and shoulders (on the left), with his back sloping down towards the north (on the right). The truncated ridge sloping down towards Redlynch is seen as* Damarri's *shortened left leg, which was bitten off by* Ganyarra *(the crocodile).*

(Photo courtesy of Michael Watt.)

with *Damarri's* resting place. *Damarri's* presence is enshrined within the landscape. In the Djabugay Story, *Damarri* killed his brother *Guyala* and lived in the Freshwater area until an old age, but in the Yidinydji and Gungganydji versions, *Guyala* returns to the north. The variations reflect the different perspectives of the different Bama groups.

The other central Storywater spirit-being present in the texture of this cultural landscape (particularly in the Barron Gorge and Stoney Creek area) is the *Burrawungal* (female water sprite). The *Burrawungal* lives in the water and is covered with slime, like a fish or an eel, but according to the Stories, although she is diminutive, she has alluring qualities similar to those of the Greek Sirens or mermaids.[38] A *Burrawungal* was captured by a warrior at a place called *Nani*, near where the Barron River divides around Kamerunga Island. The warrior made her his wife for some time, until one day she escaped through a slippery, narrow ravine, to the waters flowing from Red Peak. Above Kamerunga Island, below *Mirimbi* (referring to the crest of a cockatoo; Red Bluff) is a small hill called *Bunda Burrawungal*, which has particular significance to the Redlynch Djabugay. The

Burrawungal is often referred to as *Bunanda*, the water fairy woman, and is also known as the 'mermaid'.

In 1975, Professor Bob Dixon was told a *Burrawungal* Story in a coastal dialect by Mr Dick Moses at Yarrabah. In this Storywater a young man also caught himself a *Burrawungal*:

> He sneaked up on them, making sure that they didn't see or smell his approach, and grabbed the younger one, putting sand in his hands so that she was not able to slip through his grasp. He then took her back to his camp and heated her over a fire so that he could rub and scrape all the eel-like slime from her body. He then made her his wife and made sure she was never sent to the river for water. Eventually someone did tell her to fetch water and she went to the river, never to return.[39]

Along *Bana Wuruu* (middle Barron River)[40] from *Ngunbay* (Kuranda) to *Bubundji* (near the mouth of Freshwater Creek), numerous Djabugay villages flourished. Today, Djabugay people remember

> they had a big camp where the road and lookout is now, at the falls. That camp was there long before the railway. They were *Gurrabana* clan, *Nyinggarra*—eel is our totem. In them old days the Barron River would dry up sometimes and you could walk up and down along the river. My brother and my grandparents used to walk from tunnel 14 into Redlynch, on this side of the river (south side). You could go down near Red Bluff, and sometimes you would have to use lawyer cane like rope, 'cause it was steep. There was one camp at Kamerunga beside the crossing near where the old Kamerunga Bridge is. My mother also used to talk about Camp Oven Creek, there was a navvy camp there.[41]

The Bama took advantage of the best country to establish camps. *Bayu* (lawyer cane huts) were erected and sometimes they would build *djimurru* (large huts for thirty to forty people). These huts could be maintained over many seasons and were readily constructed when required for accommodating the large numbers associated with social gatherings, ceremony or duelling contests. Villages like *Bubundji* and *Ngunbay* were major gathering points for not only Djabugay, but also surrounding Bama representatives.[42] The utilisation of Bama walking pads, criss-crossing the district from the coast to the inland, connected people in the north, west, and south. In particular, Djabugay utilised the corridor of valleys from the Mowbray River, inland via Rifle

1.5 *Dry Barron Gorge, in the 1890s. 'In them days the Barron River would dry up sometimes and you could walk up and down along the river.' Elder, Enid Boyle.*

(Photo courtesy of John Oxley Library.)

Creek, Flaggy Creek (where Monamona Mission was later established) and on to the Barron River, on their seasonal and spiritual movements. These are well remembered by the older folk.

Some of them are centred on the Barron Gorge. Glen Williams Snr recalls:

> Above Stoney Creek Falls there's this place, an old Bama camping ground, lots of *Guln.gay* [Black Pine] grows there. Where this place is, the soil is really white and fine, like sand. There's lots of big grinding stones there, all for cracking *Guln.gay* nuts. A few of us have been in there, we used to cut timber out that way, but when we seen this place we told the boss, and we didn't end up cutting any timber from this place. Very near here, towards old Speewah my Elders told me about a place, a very special Bama place, there's an important Story there, *Bulurru*. There is this very special track, on the other side of the gorge there, this is the same way that Bunanda went, when she went back up into the creek. It is very slippery and steep you have to speak lingo when you go there, and if you do not say this special song in language, you can not go through this way. You can only go one way on this path.

Djabugay Elder, Mr Selwyn Hunter Snr remembered that 'they used to walk in from Speewah to Kuranda. The Buluwanydji mob used to walk from out Bare Hill way'.

Bare Hill's traditional name is *Bunda Dibandji*, and it contains important galleries. Buluwanydji males occupied this significant site, depending on seasonal variations. Generally, however, from the end of *Gurrabana*[43] (Wet Season), between January and June and the beginning of *Gurraminya* (Dry Season),[44] the grass was burnt and wallaby hunts conducted. Native cats, small marsupials, goannas and snakes were also obtainable.[45]

> During the dry season . . . there is an expansion of activity and this period becomes the sacred season in which aboriginal totemic life receives its most complete and intense expression.[46]

Maa or vegetable foods were abundant, but became scarcer as winter progressed. By the time of *Djindjim* (Dew Time—around July/August) of *Gurraminya*, the Bama would 'come down to the coast—for Mulgrave walnut . . . and quandong (*murrgan*)—in the winter, avoiding some of the worst of the mountain frosts and mists'.[47] James Venture Mulligan, the explorer, noted in the month of August

1.6 *Original caption: 'Food gathering track'. The myriad of Bama* djimburru *(walking pads) that criss-crossed the rugged rainforest mountains around Cairns indicates a great deal of movement by the Bama, not only for food/resources, but also for ceremonial, social and trading interactions.*

(Photo courtesy of the Historical Society of Cairns.)

1875, when traversing the Mareeba district, that 'we do not see them very often, I think they are gone down the coast'.[48] This impression was confirmed by an Aboriginal member of Mulligan's party.

Djimburru (walking tracks) cross the ranges throughout the Wet Tropics Bama lands. Well-established and well-maintained *djimburru* were important for travel to access seasonal food/resources, places and other Bama. They also linked the Storywaters, and often followed the path of these Stories, in line with associated customs—the way in which their *Gurra-Gurra* (ancestors) had before them. With this in mind, one can appreciate that there were many major thoroughfares from the coast to the Tablelands.

Wanyarra, Roy Banning, has given further evidence of widespread use of walking pads: 'Boomerang Creek, *Wangal-Wangal* [led] straight up and over the hill from Crystal Cascades, the fast way to Snake Gully, the old Veivers property. You could walk up [well] above Stoney Creek Falls.' At the middle Barron River (between the top of the Falls and Biboohra), three major creeks run off the high Lamb Range (*Bunda Djarruy Gimbul*, meaning 'Bird-Barrier Mountain') to the south and drain north into the Barron. It is the headwaters of these systems that offers a clue to the mobility of the Bama and their harnessing of the natural topography to create pathways that, to the Gadja (Europeans), accustomed to using horses, were an inaccessible mountain jungle wilderness. It is rarely more than several kilometres between the sources of these water systems. This accounts for trails joining Freshwater Creek with Shoteel Creek (which runs into Clohesy River), just south of Speewah/Snake's Creek. It has also been demonstrated that a major trail skirted the western base of Lamb Range, crossing the previously mentioned creeks, in a south-south-westerly direction and followed the Barron River to just above Tinaroo Falls, where a large Bama village was located.[49]

The people, prior to European colonisation, were a cohesive community bound together by strict religion/law/customs stemming from *Bulurru*. Its potency was functional as it maintained Bama compliance with a series of living rules. These rules were 'defined, interpreted, altered, waived (and broken) by humans, and generally by a particular set of humans—older males'.[50] So, while the impression was given that the laws were unalterable edicts from the past, they were really not quite so dogmatic. It is from this aspect that the ruling stratum emerged:[51] the *Burri-Burri* or older men.[52] Women also had a role to play, and although it tended to be subordinate to men, it was not necessarily always so; there are suggestions that some

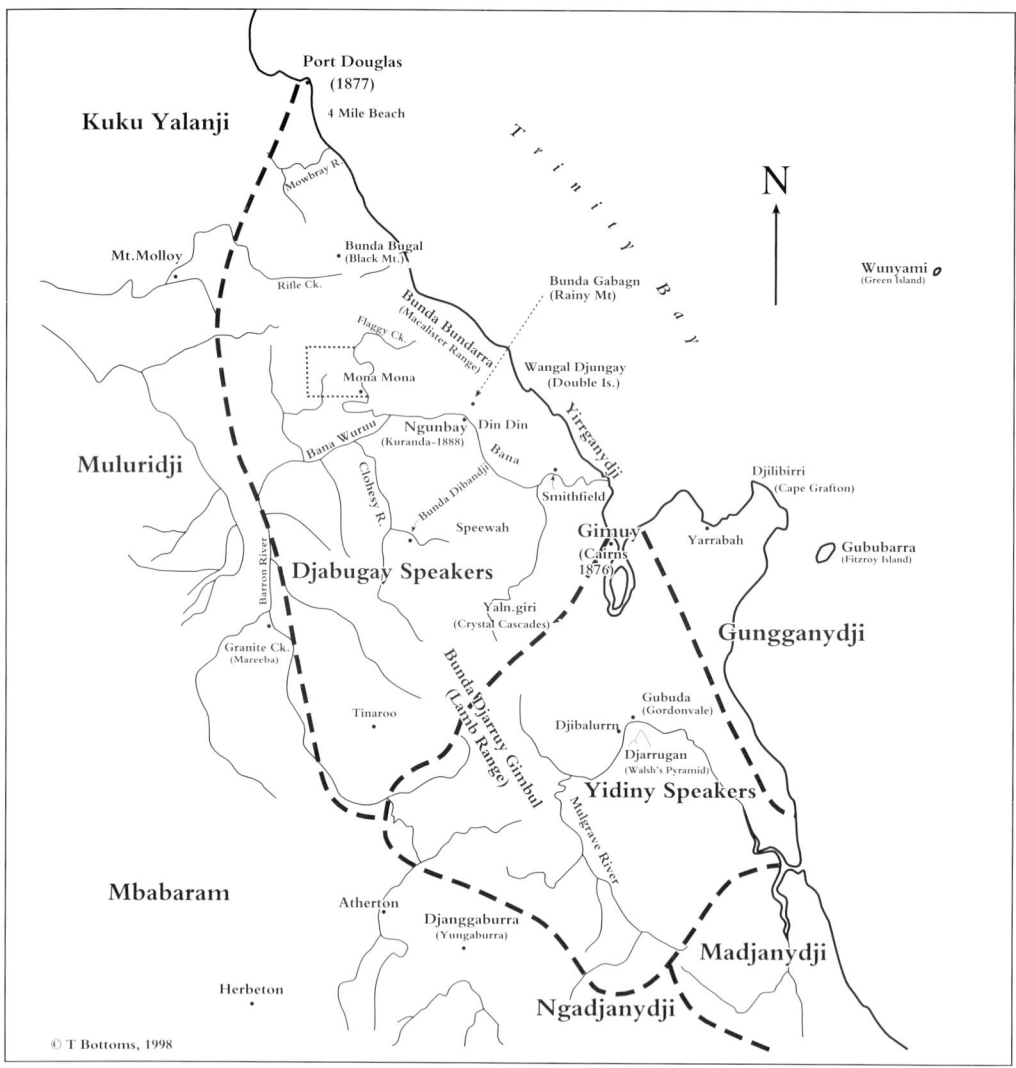

Map 2 Djabugay Bulmba

women did have 'powerful respect'. In recent historical times, women appear to have had even more status, especially since many men were away and the women had to keep on going. Ceremonial rites confirmed Bama heritage[53] and older men controlled the rites. A part of the rites involved initiating young men and women and its purpose was that they should go through an ordeal which was mentally and physically taxing. However, it was the older males who controlled the resources of *Bulurru*, and hence regulation of initiation.

1.7 Djabugay men preparing for Warrma *near Monamona in the early 1930s. Standing, third from left is Mr Steven Fagan's grandfather, Mike Shepphard. Sixth from left is Mrs Mona Fagan's grandfather, Charlie Donald. Fourth from right, with the white cross on his forehead, is Billy Duffin, the father of Mrs Flo Williams. Third from left, kneeling, is* Yuri yuri *(Sambo Mont), Mrs Williams' step-father.*
(Photo courtesy of John Oxley Library.)

The end of the ordeal was the seal of manhood and the key to a man's privilege. All this was done in a context of high excitement, secrecy and beauty. Every man who came to full manhood did so, not only with no man's hand against him, but covered by the freely given blood of a class of men who, though inherently opposed to him, depended on him as he did on them.[54]

In regard to ceremony, it would seem that rituals grew and altered in significance, although gradually.

Eric Mjoberg in 1913 noted that the structure of Bama organisation involved

standards of discipline and justice [which] form the basis of the governance of the community and the individual's actions and behaviour. The validity and respect for inherited laws and

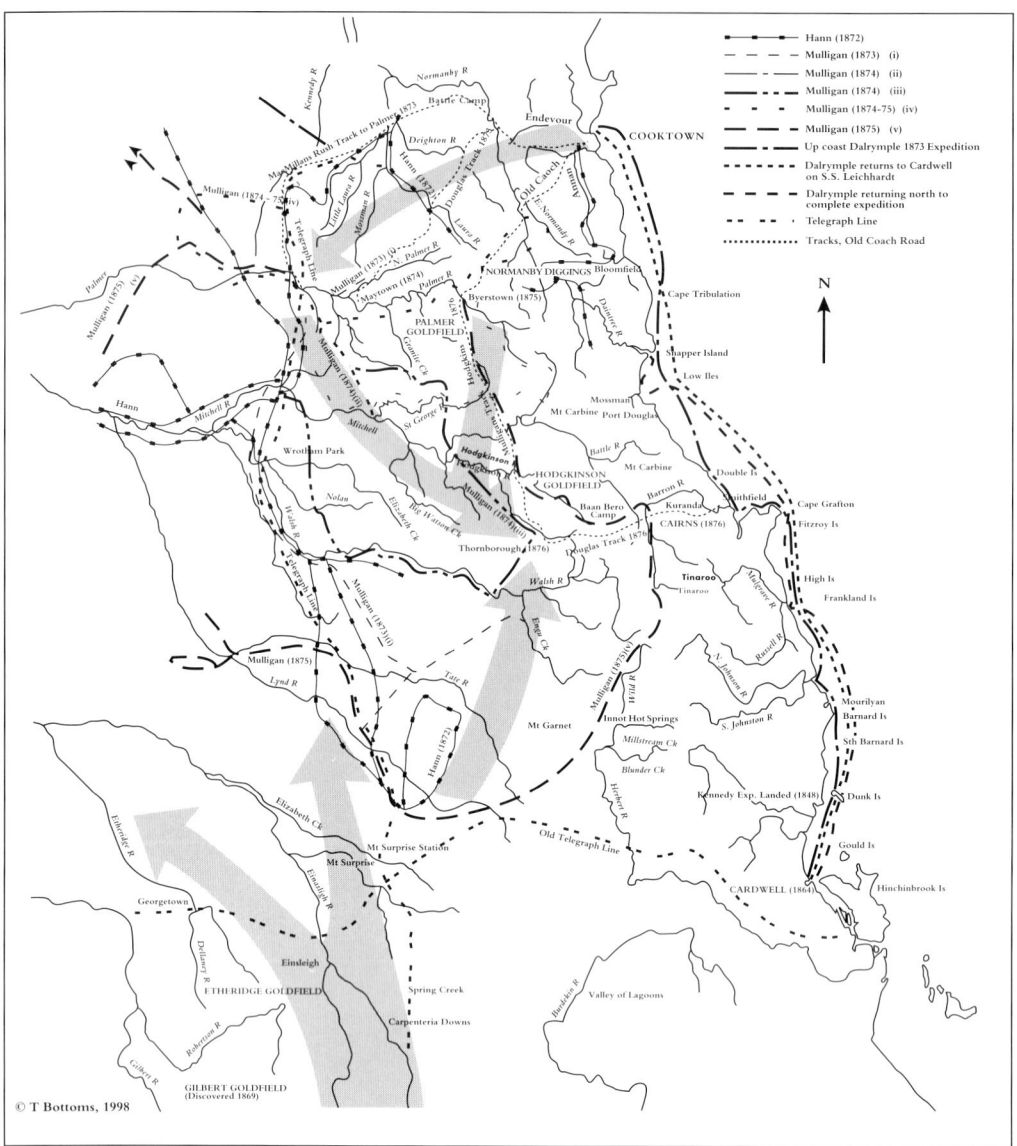

Map 3 *European exploration of Bama lands, 1870–1876*

traditions are as firmly established in the tribe, as in the individual himself. Every single action is always carefully scrutinized and, should it, in any way, exceed recognized principles, punishment will be handed out accordingly. Trespass, matrimony and pro-prietorship rights, where appropriate, are safeguarded under the strictest laws.[55]

The *Burri-Burri* (male Elders) controlled aspects of personal relations, property, aspects of diet, localities and names. However, it is necessary not to overstate this aspect, as the established belief structure and public opinion probably played as important a role as the Elders in everyday life. The distribution of food resources was dictated by a variety of influences: kin relations, transitory states (such as pregnancy or widowhood), or totemic affiliations, as well as age and sex.[56] In particular, much of the food, including the choicest items, was reserved for the *Burri-Burri*. Roth observed that a husband lived on different food from his wife (or wives) and children.[57] Like so many other Bama modes of life, there seemed to be good reason for this. Taboo foods tended to ensure continued supply, as no one source approached depletion. Male novices in particular were prohibited certain foods. It was believed that if any food taboos were broken, the availability of that whole species would be threatened, not to mention the individuals responsible, who would suffer some dire consequence (becoming diseased, treading on a poisonous fish, or some other accident). The Law would always prevail!

The metaphysical world of the *Bulurru* Storywaters and the physical world of the walking tracks of the Djabugay *Bulmba* represent a doorway to our rainforest Aboriginal Australian heritage. The connection between Storyplaces is such that there is not one particular place which has an independent value. Each place has meaningful association with other places, connected by Story. They are inextricably interlinked, just as every living thing in the *Bulmba* is related to all other living things—including human beings. This recalls other indigenous views from around the world, where it is likewise perceived that 'all things are connected'.[58]

Djabugay

2

From Bama Bulmba to Far North Queensland (1873–1912)

Captain James Cook and his crew travelled along the coastline of the sea-going Djabugay-speakers in the moonlit early hours of Monday, 11 June 1770.[1] They were quite likely unobserved. However, tales of their landing could have readily spread from the Gungganydji, whose territory the crew of the ship *Endeavour* investigated the previous afternoon while looking for water. The dispossession of the Bama began linguistically, but unintentionally, when Cook renamed *Djilibirri* (Barramundi Head), calling it Cape Grafton.[2]

There were a half dozen sea explorations along the coastline during the next 106 years.[3] But it was not until the township of Cairns was established at the end of the first week of October 1876,[4] on the site of *Gimuy*, a Bama drinking well, that Europeans truly began their invasion of the traditional lands of the Djabugay and their kindred Bama. Sub-Inspector R. A. Johnstone of the Native Mounted Police recalled their visit to the estuary of the Barron River:[5]

> The blacks were numerous, and as we entered the inlet they paddled away in their canoes and hid themselves in the small salt-water creeks. We attempted to fraternise, but they would not, though they followed us through the whole trip—in fact, we had to keep a sharp lookout when cutting through the scrub, as we

could see them occasionally, and when we were crossing a piece of open forest we could see a mob of about twenty, all armed with spears, on our tracks, and others to the right and left of us, all armed; so we were compelled to tell off two of our party to keep guard and carry the rifles of those cutting in readiness for action, and either Sub-Inspector Townsend or myself remained on the watch. It reduced our cutting party's strength, but as we also took it turn about on guard it gave a spell. The blacks were within two hundred yards of us, and making signs for us to go back, and shaking their spears at us, but they evidently remembered former troubles, as it was at False Cape [*Bunda Djadja*] that they [the Gungganydji] attacked the police boat in 1872.[6]

The Sub-Inspector's conclusion, in one sense, could very well be true, as there were close sea links between the Gungganydji and the Yirrganydji. The story of the firearms and the devastating result of their use would in all probability have been discussed around the Bama campfires. The important point is that the coastal Djabugay, the Yirrganydji, were not directly hostile; they did not attack, but let the Gadja (European)[7] intruders know they were being watched and possibly escorted. If anything, this incident demonstrated the self-control exercised by the Bama. The Gadja were in Yirrganydji territory which the Djabugay-speakers knew intimately, and it would not have been difficult for them to ambush the party. The Bama showed a diplomatic restraint which Johnstone construed as fear.

Three years before, Johnstone had visited the area as second-in-charge on the first official exploration of the 1873 Queensland North East Coast Expedition. Along the coastal stretch of *Bana Bidagarra* (coastal Barron River), the Sub-Inspector observed:

> It is a sure indication of good country when the aboriginals are numerous, as they depend entirely on Nature to provide them with the necessaries of life, and there in the valley of the Barron the jungle supplied them with fruits, roots and game in abundance.[8]

This was at the foot of the range before the ascent of the Barron Gorge in the traditional lands of the coastal Djabugay-speaking Yirrganydji. Within a week of Johnstone making these observations, the Palmer River Goldrush was underway and Cooktown was established on the banks of the river that had been renamed the Endeavour.[9] However, it was not until the discovery of the Hodgkinson Goldfield in 1876,[10] to the west of present-day Mareeba,

2.1 *Djabugay warriors with weapons unique to the rainforest Bama; the* madjay *or large shield, and* wagay, *wooden sword were used by the Bama 'for close-quarters fighting . . . in duels at the fighting ground (djirrbbi-barra bulmba) where disputes were settled . . . The shields are chopped out of the buttress roots of certain fig species . . . There are two types of large swords (wagay). One was straight and called* Gulwarra wagay; *the other was curved and known as* dubal wagay. *A wagay weighed up to 2.5 kg and measured up to 1.5 m in length . . . The wagay was swung from behind the back over the shoulder and onto the opponent's head.' (R. Duffin & R. Brim,* Ngapi Garrang Bulurru-m, All Things Come From Bulurru, *Jilli Binna, Cairns, 1992, pp. 24–29.)*

(Photo courtesy of John Oxley Library.)

that Europeans became interested in the coastal range between the Hodgkinson and Trinity Bay, looking for a closer port to the diggings—half the distance to that of Cooktown.[11] The Gadja miners trod a route through the southern part of the traditional Buluwanydji territory, north of *Bunda Djarruy Gimbul*[12] (Lamb Range), that separated them from their linguistic kinsfolk, the Yidinydji. The area from the present Mareeba, east to the coast, was 'honey-combed with . . . tracks which were easily found through the forest country'.[13] The Bama used a series of interconnecting *djimburru* (walking tracks), from the coastal area, north of *Gimuy* (Cairns) to the Mowbray River and Island Point (Port Douglas) and then west to the other side of *Bunda Bundarra*

Courtesy of the Queensland Department of Natural Resources

Map 4 *1877 plan of track from Thornborough to Cairns*

(Cassowary Range or Macalister Range). Main thoroughfares criss-crossed the Djabugay *Bulmba* (homelands), as they also did with neighbouring Bama tribes. Similarly, major village sites were located at prominent food resource areas, close to water. *Ngunbay*, 'Place of Platypus', which became the Gadja settlement of Kuranda, was one such important gathering place. Elder, Grandma Flo Williams, recalls that the area was called '*Gurii-anda*' and that Bama from here used to traverse the *djimburru* (walking tracks) down to the bottom of the range near present–day Smithfield. The white people had trouble pronouncing '*Gurii-anda*' and so called it 'Kuranda'.[14]

William Smith, John Doyle and party had made several unsuccessful attempts to find a route through to the Hodgkinson from the coast. However,

> On Tuesday, Sept. 19th, Smith and party climbed the range on foot, probably following blacks' tracks along the spur through which now passes No. 9 tunnel on the Kuranda railway. From there they crossed Stoney Creek and then tramped on to Grove Creek which they recognized from a previous expedition and finally on to Thornborough, seventy miles away and arrived on Thursday, 21st Sept., just two days after the initial ascent.[15]

The first direct European reference to the inland Djabugay-speakers occurred when Warden St George telegrammed his superiors in August 1876, about John Doyle and party who searched from the inland for a route to the coastal area that became 'Cairns'.[16] He described the Bama at the top of the range as being 'bad', basically because they opposed the Gadja passage through their territory. On another attempt, this time from the coast, Doyle, Evans, Geary and McCord in mid-October crossed the coastal range using part of Smith's track, and came to a gorge where 'probably the mightiest waterfall in the Australian colonies' was observed.[17] The Djabugay-speakers called this *Din Din*, but to the newcomers it became the Barron Falls. On their return to Thornborough, Doyle and party met with members of the Buluwanydji, 'and presents [were] interchanged, but afterwards they showed up with their arms and looked like fighting, a few shots, however, dispersed them'.[18]

Meanwhile, Sub-Inspector Douglas[19] had set off from Thornborough on 17 September and 'at what was later known as Groves Creek, his further progress was blocked for horses, and a camp was made. He probably sent some of his troopers to look for black's [sic] tracks, knowing nothing of course of Smith's success'.[20]

2.2 Din Din *(Barron Falls). Street Creek Camp (see 2.13) was located just over the ridge, seen above the Falls in the middle of the photo.*

(Photo courtesy of the Windmill Cafe, Kuranda.)

The expedition continued through the 'scrub' or rainforest territory of the Djabugay, and observed along the way was

> a splendid black's hut, made of palm leaves, with fine doors to it. Heaps of nuts outside proved that it was a favourite camp, amid the solitude of an almost impenetrable forest. The track from the first open spur goes down into a very steep creek, and after about two hours travelling through timber scrub, bad gullies and pinches, we came to a pinch which winded us all, and on arriving at the top were gratified by the sight of the sea and a large river winding to the base of the spur on which we were standing. From this we descended sheer down about half-a-mile, and after considerable swearing, leaning, slipping and blowing, emerged suddenly on a splendid running stream 40 yards wide, with both sides covered with mountain scrub.[21]

This, with probable variations, became the Douglas Track. It is interesting to note that Smith and Douglas' explorations utilised Bama

23

walking pads. Seven days prior to the above report the *Cooktown Herald* wrote: 'The blacks are said to be very numerous and daring, and have already speared two horses of the 180, which came with Mr Smith.'[22] Correspondents recorded the contentious debate over whether either of the two tracks were any good, particularly for wheeled vehicles. Certainly by mid-November 1876, within a month of establishing the new settlements of Cairns and (old) Smithfield (located on the northern bank of the Barron River, roughly a kilometre downstream from the junction with Freshwater Creek), work had begun on improving the access to the tracks going up Barron Gorge and on to Thornborough. Conflict between the traditional owners and the invading Gadja was bound to occur. It is therefore not surprising that

> the road party up the Barron came across a strong party of blacks, apparently prepared to check their further advance, and on looking back . . . another party of fifteen or twenty were observed sneaking up as though bent on no good. The road party counted but four well armed men, and so after speaking to the poor misguided savages in the language usual in such circumstances, they returned to camp. Since this first brush I understand the blacks have been twice interviewed by the same party, and that on each occasion there was an interchange of compliments, without any casualties, however, on the side of the white men.[23]

One must assume that there were Bama casualties, but to what extent it is difficult to judge, except that the oblique nature of the report and the repeated negative interaction suggested the results did not bode well for the Djabugay. The precedent of violent behaviour by European miners had already been set on the Palmer River goldfield; N. Kirkman explained that traditionally this has been interpreted as an 'extraordinary degree of ferocity and hostility on the part of local Aborigines'. Kirkman challenges this interpretation by claiming 'the outbreak of hostilities can be precisely dated and was invariably the result of acts of deliberate provocation on the part of Europeans'.[24]

The tracks were in frequent use by Europeans by August 1877, for it was reported that the principal trade was 'carried on by water, by means of small steamers and lighters up the Barron River . . . The great Government road from the Hodgkinson comes in here [old Smithfield], and nearly all the packers stop here and get their supplies, very few of them going into Cairns, as there is no grass for their horses . . .'[25] While it is likely that the author is probably being sarcastic about the 'great Government road', there can be no doubt that miners were landing at Trinity Bay to make their way inland to Thornborough and the goldfields. John Winfield recalled his father, Patrick, anchoring at Trinity Bay, where

> the men could not get into the small boats fast enough. To avoid swamping it was decided to take their possessions first with a few men to look after same. This process was too slow for some who swam and waded through the mud to shore with rain falling most of the time. Once ashore, without delay, many started walking along the newly cut track. Others stayed until next morning, being nearly eaten alive by sandflies and mosquitoes. The new track was mostly loose sand and mangrove mud covered by

2.3 Initiated Djabugay men and uninitiated boys in the Kuranda area, around 1890. Bulurru or '[t]he Storytime is inscribed on the body of the land as it was upon the very bodies of the initiated who bore the signs of their making wadirr *(initiatory cicatrices) on shoulders, chest and stomach.' (R. Banning & M. Quinn,* Bulurru Storywater, *Cairns, 1990, p. v.) Note the* wagay *(wooden sword) which is unique to the rainforest Bama.*

(Photo courtesy of the Historical Society of Cairns.)

undergrowth. Those that left directly found their loads too heavy so discarded all surplus such as tents, flies, clothing, picks, etc, which were scattered along the track. The hazards impeded their progress and they were not able to get to Smithfield at the foot of the range. In camping on the track the leeches were as bad as the mosquitoes and the men had a terrible night in the rain. They climbed the range next day, weary and tired. That evening when my Dad and his party arrived after a strenuous day to the banks of the Barron, they found the leading party drying their possessions. All resolved on an enjoyable night's sleep away from pests. Before going to sleep the dingoes started howling and many thought this might herald an attack from the blacks. They then decided to scatter from the many fires they had lit and risk the snakes and bull-ants disturbed at the foot of the trees . . . On the third day they were near the boundaries of the new field.[26]

Between 1878 and the early 1880s, there are numerous reports from the Native Mounted Police of 'outrages' and 'depredations' that had been committed by the 'bad Blacks of the north'.[27] 'Outrages' usually referred to spearings or challenges to the invading whites, while 'depredations' involved the stealing of property or crops, or the killing of cattle.[28] In 1880, Inspector Isley's half-yearly report to the Acting Commissioner of Police stated that crime had not increased and that the force at his disposal was sufficient, except for guarding gold escorts. Rather cryptically, Isley observed that the

> Blacks have been unusually troublesome in the neighbourhood of Cairns and Smithfield . . . [D]epredations have also been committed by them in the Thornborough portion of the District, and as these outrages frequently happen at the same time in places wide apart from each other, the Barron River Detach[ment] of Native Police has not been strong enough to cope with the difficulty.[29]

Isley implies that there is some form of co-operation between the Kuku Djungan, Muluridji and Djabugay/Yidiny-speakers, whom he terms the 'Blacks'. Had their pilfering and spearing tactics developed into something more determined? Reynolds has observed for other areas that '[f]or the groups in question the constraints of custom had been circumvented, [and] they had moved from feud to warfare'.[30]

It is interesting to note what the Commissioner of Police, W. E. Parry-Okedon, observed in 1897 with regard to depredations: 'I think that in many instances they are not conscious of interfering

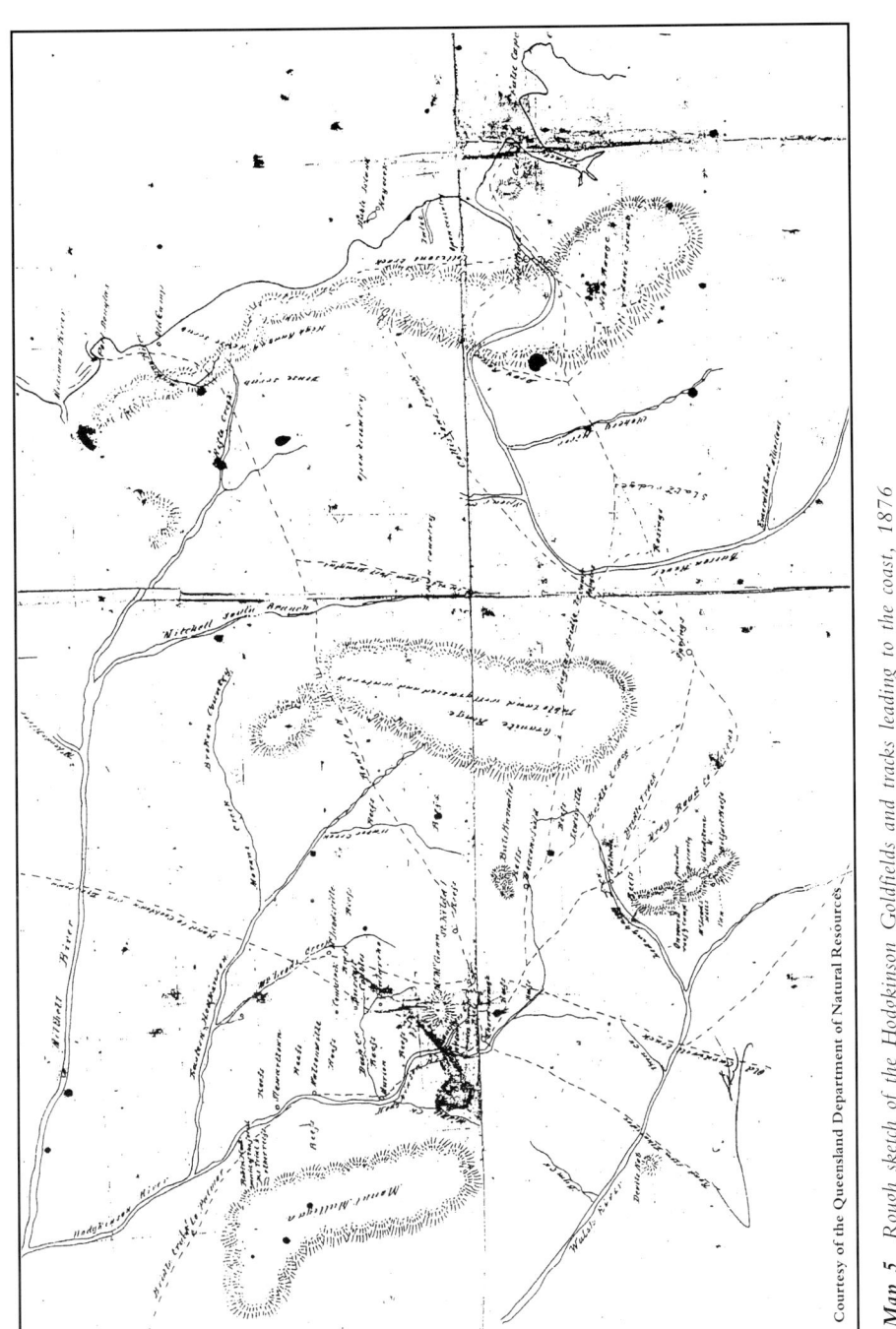

Map 5 Rough sketch of the Hodgkinson Goldfields and tracks leading to the coast, 1876

with property not belonging to them, but regard cattle roaming in the bush as food natural, and as such their lawful prey, and in many instances there is much contributory neglect of their stock on the part of the owners.'[31] There are actually only two reports of Djabugay spearing travellers or packers, one incident in 1878,[32] and another in 1879,[33] both at the Middle Crossing, close to where Kuranda is now located. Both resulted in wounding. There are only two reports of individuals being killed by the Djabugay, one of seven Chinese travellers was speared and killed in 1882,[34] somewhere between Granite Creek and Cairns, and the second, a settler, at Myola in 1890.[35]

Cairns, and the use of the inland tracks, began to decline after the 'Bump Track' from Thornborough to Port Douglas was opened.[36] This track was a part of the myriad of Bama walking paths that criss-crossed the region and linked coastal and inland groups to one another for trade, ceremonial and family interactions.[37] In July, William Wade 'was speared by the blacks in the vicinity of the scrub near Island Point . . . [although] he was progressing favorably [sic]', and D. Clark reported two of his horses being speared at Rifle Creek, where '[t]he blacks are becoming troublesome along the track. Their fires are frequently visible, and their cooee can be heard constantly. The tall spear-grass completely hides them from view . . .'[38] In early September 1877, the first pack team reached Salisbury, renamed Port Douglas in November. It was from here one month later that the first mail was delivered to the goldfields.[39] J. W. Collinson, the noted Cairns historian, observed that '[t]he only road available for wheeled traffic was to Port Douglas, and this port enjoyed all the prosperity brought about by the new rush. Still the packers used the track to Cairns to some extent, though the years 1880 and 1881 were the years of the greatest depression in Cairns . . .'[40] Further difficulties arose with the disastrous flood of *Bana Bidagarra* (coastal Barron River) in 1879, when the old town of Smithfield 'was swept away in an avalanche of waters'.[41] Some claimed it was 'divine retribution' for the sinful ways of the inhabitants of the town. The Bama would probably have agreed, but on account of the Gadja's transgression of Bama *Bulurru* (Religion/Law/Storywater), rather than a white man's myth created after the tragic murder/suicide that occurred later in the year.[42] Despite the demise of old Smithfield, and the eclipsing of Cairns by Port Douglas, the tracks remained in use by Europeans, if only for pack-horse teams.

Meanwhile the clan groups of the Djabugay were still traversing

2.4 Probably taken from Red Bluff on the newly constructed Cairns–Kuranda railway line up the Barron Gorge in the 1890s. 'Old' Smithfield on the coastal Barron River (Bana Bidagarra) was located near the top left of this photograph. Today's Lake Placid is where the flooded river begins to curve to the east (left). Kamerunga is situated in the clearing on the right, just around the bend of the river. This was the base for operations in the construction of the railway. Cairns is located on the other side of the two hills (Whitfield Range) in the distance.

(Photo courtesy of John Oxley Library.)

the wide corridor from *Bana Wuruu* (middle Barron River), along the valleys around Flaggy, Big Rooty and Rifle Creeks, north to the Mowbray River and down to its mouth, and the coast.[43] Here they erected their *bayu* (huts)

> at the junction of Collards Creek and the Mowbray. The frames were sticks and lawyer cane, and were covered with bark from the Melaleuca (Titree) which grew along the banks of the river. The camps were very neat, and were dry when it rained. They didn't stay much longer than a few months at any one campsite, before they moved on.[44]

The Mulgrave River goldrush at Goldsborough, in Malanbarra Yidinydji territory, helped sustain the struggling settlement of Cairns. Similarly, the opening of a pack-track to transport tin from Herberton on the Tablelands to the Mulgrave Valley and on to the headwaters of Trinity Inlet, as well as the Tinaroo pack-track to Groves selection and on to Cairns,[45] both assisted the finances of the fledgling Gadja community. However, the 'Bump Track' was becoming difficult to traverse during *Gurrabana* (Wet Season) and, in 1882, the region experienced a particularly long and heavy Wet. Herberton was unable to bring in supplies and famine threatened the settlement's existence. This led the citizens of Herberton to lobby for an all-season railway to the coast. Both Port Douglas and Cairns began to promote themselves as the best port for the proposed railway inland. Thus it was that Christie Palmerston was engaged to find a railway route to the coast.[46] In July 1882, he and his erstwhile Bama mate, Pompo, explored the Barron Gorge for a likely route. It was along an open spur, now pierced by No. 13 tunnel, and below Smith's track, that Palmerston found 'a large native track . . . This spur does not appear to be half the height of Douglas's track, or Smiths [sic], and no steeper, it certainly would have made a better pack track than either of them.'[47] Christie did not think that there was any suitable route via the Barron Gorge, as 'it will require engineering and skill, to surmount the range here',[48] and on this point he was undoubtedly right. Nevertheless, his comments on the well-used Bama walking pad confirm the Bama's use of their *Bulmba* (homeland) in this area.

It took two years for the railway surveyors to complete their assessments and submit their findings to the Queensland Government. In March 1884, the choice favoured the Barron Valley Gorge, which caused great indignation in Port Douglas and Mourilyan Harbour (on the coast, about twelve kilometres south-east of Geraldton, which became Innisfail in 1910) who were vying with Cairns to be the railway port to the hinterland.[49] Nevertheless, the die had been cast, and the future of Cairns was now assured, and so was that of the Bama.

While the Djabugay clans were unaware of what the Gadja intended for the *Bulmba*, they were apparently not content with the arrival of Gadja settlers. In the valley of the 'Singing Waters' near the area of Freshwater Creek, the Bama were 'pilfering' items from newly arrived settlers, one of whom stated that 'he will be compelled to abandon his homestead unless an example is made of these blacks by punishing them'.[50] *Yilbong* of the Undanbi[51] gave an indigenous perspective on this to Tom Petrie, an early settler north of Brisbane, when he explained 'that he saw no harm in stealing because the white man had "taken his country" and they "should give something for it"'.[52]

In May 1886, construction of the railway began from Cairns.[53] Five months later Surveyor Stuart found a new practical track up the

2.5 *John Robb, the railway contractor 'had gangs working simultaneously at sites over the greater length of this section and established small camps at each site where enough comparatively flat land could be found to pitch a few tents'. (A. Broughton,* Cairns Range Railway 1886–1891, *Historical Society of Cairns, 1991, p. 27.) This navvies camp was perched on the edge of the Barron Gorge near Red Bluff (below and north of Glacier Rock). See Map 6.*

(Photo courtesy of the Historical Society of Cairns.)

Barron Gorge, but it was too late to be developed, as the railway line had already been started.[54] Meanwhile, the Native Mounted Police were in action in the district. The editor of the *Cairns Post* wrote: 'We are glad to see Sgt. Whelan down amongst us once more with his troops. The blacks have not been nearly as troublesome since he commenced his patrols some long time back.'[55] Nevertheless, local white settlers like Mrs Rose Veivers 'told many stories of how pleased and excited the Veivers' family were when they could smell the smoke of the fires, lit by migrating Aborigines travelling from Freshwater valley to Speewah'.[56]

In May 1887, the centre of operations chosen by the railway contractor, John Robb, at Barronville, became 'Kamerunga, a native name for the new township on the Barron River'.[57] Throughout this period, Robb 'had gangs working simultaneously at sites over the

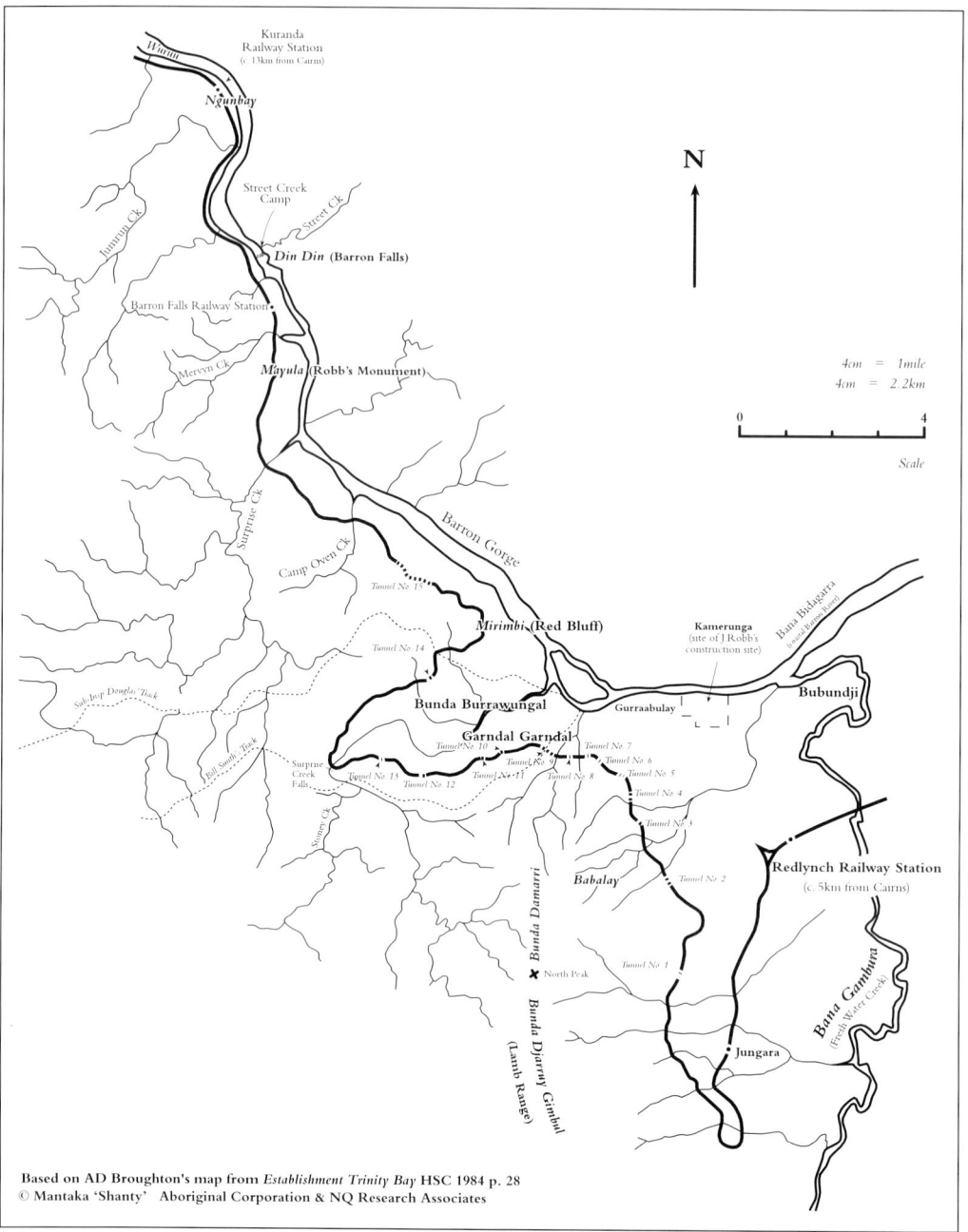

Map 6 *Range Railway and Barron Gorge*

greater length of this section and established small camps at each site where enough comparatively flat land could be found to pitch a few tents'.[58] Meanwhile, the Bama were 'becoming an intolerable nuisance to some of the people along the second section'.[59] The first section of the railway line was opened on 8 October 1887.[60] The second section of the railway was from Redlynch at the base of the range to Myola, about four kilometres beyond the current station at Kuranda, and it is here where the pack tracks via the Barron Gorge are all located. It was also here that navvies getting hickory logs for the railway were forced to leave one man on guard in camp 'otherwise every scrap of food is taken by the thieving rascals. A little "Rough on Rats" judiciously disposed amongst some damper would effectually stop these annoyances'.[61] By September the Police Department had taken over Archibald Meston's property as a site for a police camp, presumably to deal with Bama 'depredations'. Certainly in November, in response to garden produce being stolen, *Cairns Post* readers were informed that 'Sgt. Whelan's attention is to be directed to dispersing these trouble-some customers'.[62] It is not particularly surprising that Djabugay were stealing food from the settlers, as their traditional food gathering and hunting areas were being taken over by the Gadja settlers. Similarly, in early 1888, there were up to 700 men working on the second section,[63] and the impact they had on the tracks and food resources of the Bama can be imagined.[64] Near Stoney Creek, railway workers' tents were ransacked and it was reported that part of the thievery was by blacks, one of whom was caught at Kamerunga. He had a sovereign and half a sovereign in his possession, and it was observed that the Bama were becoming aware of the '. . . purchasing power of money'.[65] The following month more thefts were reported near tunnel no. 12,[66] close-by to Stoney Creek.

> During the construction, the navvies' camps were formed at every cutting and tunnel and even comparatively narrow ledges became the sites of stores, some of them not catering for the needs of the men in the way of groceries and drapery!! At Number 3 tunnel, Stoney Creek, the springs at the foot of the Glacier Rock, Camp Oven Creek and Gray Pocket (Rainbow Creek) just above the falls, were, in their day, busy and thriving townships . . . 1,500 men in all were engaged in various activities associated with the building of the line.[67]

The impact on the Bama of the increasing numbers of miners and timber-getters was becoming apparent throughout the region.

2.6 *Construction camp 'with workers' tents and shanty alongside a cutting near the Springs (see Map 6). In the building of this railway the men had no equipment other than their own skills, shovels, horses and blasting powder' (Broughton, 1991, p. 12). This view is looking south-west, with Glacier Rock above the railway cutting. The Douglas track comes down from the saddle to the right of the Rock.*

(Photo courtesy of the Historical Society of Cairns.)

The Queenslander reported in December 1877 that the Palmer River 'blacks' 'seem half-starved, and recent advice from the Hodgkinson describe the aboriginals there . . . [as] . . . suffering from famine. The white men occupy their only hunting grounds, and in default . . . they are in a manner compelled to eat horses and bullocks'.[68] The following year the Commissioner of Police reported:

> The whole coast from the Mulgrave to the Mossman is studded with timber-getters and settlers, by whom the blacks are disturbed and prevented from obtaining their natural food in that direction, while on the other side of the range, the country is all occupied by small cattle stations, which again cut them off from their hunting, freshwater fishing grounds. The intervening scrub is small, affording but scanty supply of fruits in their season, and the natives are literally starving.[69]

Unfortunately, these reports fail to mention the mental anguish caused by the destruction of spiritual links to the *Bulmba* and the

2.7 Original caption: 'Barron River Police Camp, 1888'. The site of Baan Bêro was chosen by Inspector Isley in 1877, six kilometres north-north-west of the present Biboohra. Sub-Inspector Alex Douglas was in charge. In 1887, Bishop Gilbert White described the officer's house as standing 'on top of a hill, about 100 feet high [about 30 metres], which has been cleared of timber. Below are the quarters of the troopers and the stables. Close by is a large paddock with two large lagoons covered with waterfowl. The view is superb. You see over a great plain covered with trees to the blue mountains, which rise fifteen or twenty miles away on every side.' Sub-Inspector Garraway was Officer in Charge in 1888. See Chapter 2, note 71.

(Photo courtesy of John Oxley Library from the *North Queensland Register*, 25 March 1933.)

contributing factor of Bama demoralisation. There are few official reports of European retribution upon the Bama. At least two dispersals took place in 1878, one near Smithfield, and the other south-east of the Barron Police Camp (in the area near Biboohra/Granite Creek (Granite Creek became Mareeba when the railway reached there in 1893)).[70] Baan Bêro was the name of the police camp, established by Sub-Inspector Douglas in 1877,[71] which was centrally located to protect travellers going to and from the Hodgkinson.[72] In the same year, eleven kilometres away on the south bank of the Barron, John Atherton established his selection called 'Emerald End' (near the junction of Emerald Creek and the Barron River, not far from the future Mareeba). Within two weeks of the latest dispersal, Atherton too was complaining about the 'repeated incursions of the blacks' at Tinaroo. He claimed that the tinfield that he recently discovered would have to be abandoned, and that 'the road that has been newly cut through the scrub, from Tinaroo to the Inlet, ten miles from Cairns, will become untraversable from the want of proper police protection'.[73] However, the road via the Mulgrave Atherton refers to was seldom used by packers from Tinaroo. They appear to have utilised a track going north-east to Groves selection,[74] then, depending on weather conditions, via the government dray road to Cairns in the Dry Season, but via the Douglas Track to Cairns during the Wet. One and a half years after Atherton's letter to the Colonial Secretary, Sub-Inspector Carr reported to the Commissioner of Police that on 13 August 1881, he and his troopers had 'dispersed blacks [Buluwanydji] at the head of the Clohesy River for killing cattle', which suggests that this was at the behest of Atherton, as this was a part of the area over which he ran his herds.[75] Nevertheless, Bama pilfering of Gadja settlers' goods was particularly vexatious and caused great anxiety and fear amongst the new arrivals. However, Bama oral history and oblique public references recall the tragedies which were perpetrated.

During the early 1880s an Irish prospector turned pack-horse carrier, Patrick Molloy, worked the Port Douglas–Herberton road.[76] He and his wife established a home at the top of the range near the convergence of the traditional lands of the Djabugay and Kuku Yalanji.[77] At one stage he lost eight of his draught horses to the Djabugay. Molloy and a party of Native Mounted Police and some white settlers tracked the Djabugay group to *Bunda Bugal* (Black Mountain), at the head of Rifle Creek, where their 'camp was quickly surrounded [and] the blacks who showed fight were dispersed and taught a lesson that cured their taste for horse flesh for a considerable

2.8 *Coastal Djabugay utilised* djimburru *(walking pads) from Island Point (Port Douglas) along the coast, south to the Mowbray River valley, up and over the range to Rifle and Spring Creeks, and along a corridor of valleys to* Bana Wuruu *(middle Barron River). 'The northern Djabugay were described by Archibald Meston as the old Port Douglas tribe [as well as] a few of the Mowbray River blacks [who] are camped a short distance along the beach from Port Douglas.'*

(Photo courtesy of the N. H. Rex Collection from *Queenslander*, 17 January 1920, p. 23, photographer Keith Kennedy.)

time. In fact some of them lost it altogether'.[78] This understatement belies the seriousness of what had occurred and conveniently over-looks the reasoning behind Bama 'depredations'.

An early white 'pioneer', Grannie Reynolds, recalled when her family settled in the Mowbray River valley 'there was no trouble whatever with the Chabbuki [Djabugay] tribe. Another tribe . . . camped at White Cliffs, reportedly a very ferocious tribe was the Yirkandja [Yirrganydji] tribe, who roamed as far as Spring Creek area'[79]—the valley running north to the Mowbray, about four kilometres from White Cliffs. It would appear that the 'ferocity' of the Djabugay-speaking Yirrganydji may have had something to do with them spearing cattle and taking

> what meat they wanted and leav[ing] the carcasses to rot. After all threats and pleas had failed, some of the farmers went to the camp and fired shots in the air. The tribe fled the area. The next morning, Mr Robbins went to the camp and found a little baby girl that had been left in the camp. He took her home and a Mossman family reared her.[80]

2.9 *Taken about 1920 near the mouth of the Mowbray River, south of Port Douglas. 'From the Mossman River down to Cape Grafton the dug-out is cut very very square at either extremity . . . The space between the gunwale is extremely narrow . . . and yet I have known five or six people at one time travelling all the way from Port Douglas to beyond Cairns . . . This variety of dug-out can be made from at least five kinds of timber, and will range up to fifteen or sixteen feet in length . . . The [Gunnganydji] . . . of Cape Grafton speak of the float as bunul, the local term for mullet, indicative of its habit of skimming along the surface of the water.'*

(W. E. Roth, *North Queensland Ethnography*, Bulletin 14, 1910, pp. 14–15.) (Photo courtesy of John Oxley Library.)

Bama oral history tells of a massacre in the Spring Creek valley where police from the Police Reserve, located on the south side of the mouth of the Mowbray River,[81] herded people into the valley, up where the old lime crusher is, on the eastern side. They chased them up to where the lime quarry now is and killed them.[82]

Similar factors seem to have been operating with the infamous incident now called the Speewah Massacre. This appears to have taken place about mid-1890.[83] Probably the most notable Gadja selector in the district was John Atherton. The sudden increase in Gadja encroachment on Bama *Bulmba* led to conflict, particularly when Atherton stocked the district with his cattle. He 'estimated his average loss as a bullock a day for five years, and once or twice a spear was aimed at him'.[84] The losses are undoubtedly an exaggeration. Certainly in 1884, Atherton was complaining in the *Cairns Post* about his great losses and how he applied to Sub-Inspector Carr of the Native Mounted Police for protection, 'but only received in reply an intimation that he and his troopers were stationed in the district to protect the blacks, not to punish them. I am not sure if this is really the case, but if it is I fail to see what use he is to the white population'.[85] Apparently the authorities agreed with him, for the Native Mounted Police did respond to a later complaint by Atherton. The Djabugay today tell the story of how John Atherton engaged Bama to drive a herd of cattle over the Douglas track, with a promise of a bullock for payment. Upon completion of the job, they were offered a *yarraman*—a horse. The Bama were offended and disgruntled, refused the horse and took a bullock instead. They travelled to *Guwulu*, old Speewah, near today's Snake Gully, where they prepared the slaughtered beast for *bayngga* (earth oven—hot rocks). During the

2.10 *Coastal Djabugay-speakers, probably Yirrganydji, with the Cairns–Kuranda railway in the background, cut into the range going up the Barron Gorge. Notice the impact of Gadja settlement with their fencing demarcation of land in stark contrast to the Bama Bulurru 'world view'.*

(Photo courtesy of John Oxley Library.)

preparation, one of the stones burnt a young girl, Buttercup, and her mother, Minnie, took her to the river to wash and cool the burn. Whilst down the river, they heard gunshots and looked towards the camp and saw their people being shot down by the Native Mounted Police. In terror they fled for their lives down to Crystal Cascades and the sanctuary of a white selector's family, that of the American, Andrew Banning.[86]

It is quite feasible that other similar incidents may have occurred. One such unconfirmed incident is the Black Water Lagoon Massacre,[87] which is believed to have taken place west of Wright's Crossing, south-west of Mona Mona. Another which Elders recall was at Mama's Camp[88] on Flaggy Creek and yet another at Balilee (also on Flaggy Creek), where cattlemen believed the Bama to be killing and eating their bullocks. Grandma Flo remembers that after this episode, 'the water ran red with blood'.[89] An insight into the tragedies suffered by the close-knit Bama family groups can be glimpsed when one

2.11 Mayula *(Robb's Monument). The Storywater for this refers to a man and a woman breaching etiquette by having an illegal relationship. They were both from the* Gurrabana *(Wet Season) moiety (or budjanydji). The Gurra-Gurra (ancestors) punished them by turning them to stone (personal communication, Elders, Lyn and Marita Hobbler, 21 September 1998). The rock on the right was taller, but apparently was damaged during the construction of the Cairns–Kuranda railway. The Gadja ignored Bama heritage and named it in honour of John Robb, the railway contractor for the second section.*

(Photo courtesy of John Oxley Library.)

2.12 Mayula *(Robb's Monument) and the newly completed Cairns–Kuranda Railway with the associated destruction of Djabugay* Bulmba, *and desecration of the* Bulurru *(Religion/Law/Storywater) path of* Budaadji *(carpet snake/rainbow serpent).*

(Photo courtesy of John Oxley Library.)

considers the psychological ramifications of the 1996 Port Arthur Massacre in Tasmania.

In 1874 the Queensland Government received recommendations from their Land Commissioners that £350 000 a year of the £1.4 million derived from the sale of Crown land be 'set aside and held for the Government in trust for the benefit of those who are left of the tribes who formerly held these lands in possession'.[90] This thinking was easily forgotten because in 1877, when the first land sales were held in Cairns, no thought was given to the suggestion of the 1874 report.

Whilst the railway construction crews worked steadily on carving their way up the Barron Gorge, desecrating the path of *Budaadji*, the sacred Storywater Carpet Snake, the Bama were becoming increasingly aware that the Gadja invaders were here to stay. The Djabugay, along with other Bama tribes, were feeling the impact of Gadja settlement on their traditional homelands. By 1885, there were some sixteen selections taken up in the Kuranda area,[91] and at least twenty-six in the district the following year,[92] when the Cairns–Myola section of the railway commenced. In 1888, lands around the Clohesy River were opened for selection.[93] The fledgling Gadja settlement at the Middle Crossing had been surveyed for a new township called 'Kuranda', and within a

2.13 Identified as Street Creek Camp by Elder, Selwyn Hunter. In the background is Bana Wuruu
(middle Barron River), upstream from Din Din *(Barron Falls), which is located downstream to the left. The
lattice framework for a* bayu *(hut) has been completed (centre), and is ready for the next stage of protective
layering. Around the early 1900s.*

(Photo courtesy of the Historical Society of Cairns.)

month the Jum Rum Hotel had been opened.

The growing destruction of the *Bulmba* threatened not only the
Bama's food supply, but also the spiritual links. In each clan estate,
individual Bama had rights and responsibilities to look after particular
tracts of land.[94] This also involved the 'ownership' of individual
species which had association with *Bulurru* and the *Gurra-Gurra*
(ancestors), whether it be a particular tree or a totemic link with a
member of the animal or insect species. The disappearance of these
links with Gadja land clearance, undoubtedly threw the surviving
Bama into mourning, and disheartening mayhem. It was the all-
encompassing nature of Bama *Bulurru* that Gadja have failed to
understand. However, it must be acknowledged that there were some
Gadja who understood the Bama's predicament. One Professor
Rentoul who visited Kuranda in 1890 considered that

> murders by the aborigines . . . are prompted generally by a desire
> for revenge either for outraged womankind, for the countenanced

interference with the black gins, or for blacks who have been shot. In other cases the blacks have been wronged by selectors without any bad intention. For instance, the selectors in clearing their land cut down food trees which were of great value, and in some places, areas where the aborigines used to spend a couple of months gathering nuts, feasting, and merry-making, have been quite denuded of the food-bearing trees. The Government gave the selectors the land; the blacks were driven off it and got nothing in return.[95]

Professor Rentoul went on to say that '[t]he selectors . . . strongly urge that the Government should make some reserve as a compensation to the blacks for the land taken from them'.[96]

By 1891 the Cairns–Kuranda Range Railway had been completed[97] and a renewed interest in the lands along the railway line led to a further increase in Gadja settlement.[98] No doubt the massive flooding of *Bana Wuruu* (middle Barron River) in the same year[99] was interpreted by the Djabugay as 'divine retribution' for Gadja transgression of Bama *Bulmba* and sacredness of the *Bulurru* Storywaters.

The traditional village site near Myola[100] was still in full use in August 1891, when the Reverend J. B. Gribble took the train to Myola, for '[a]fter service Mr Rudd took me to the camp in the jungle not far from the township. The Myalls were holding a corroboree. They were all in war paint and feathers . . .'[101] In late November, Lady Eileen Knox, referring to the same village, recorded:

> It was a very picturesque scene; the rich, dark brown of the natives and their huts, the reds of the dying fires and films of blue smoke as they curled upwards against the dark background of forest jungle, and in the foreground the sheen of sunlight on the river, where the lithe figure of a native boy was dexterously paddling a little canoe to the opposite side, all combined to form a picture. Wild beautiful nature shut me in on every side.[102]

During this period, between twenty and fifty miners were sluicing the waters of Freshwater Creek[103] for gold, and apparently also tried their luck in the vicinity of the railway line up the gorge. Their efforts merely added to the Bama's perception that they were being invaded. At this stage there were some 7000 Gadja settlers in the Cairns region,[104] and males outnumbered females by about three to one. Prior to the coming of the Gadja, the Bama of the Cairns

2.14 In 1904, when this was taken, members of the Djabugay had adopted European dress, but still lived in traditional bayu *villages along* Bana Wuruu *(middle Barron River), from* Din Din *(Barron Falls) upstream to Myola and Mareeba. This is Street Creek Camp. The barbed wire fence possibly has an unintentional symbolic significance.*

(Photo courtesy of the Historical Society of Cairns.)

region numbered between 4000 and 5000.[105] These numbers rapidly declined with the advent of new diseases, addictions, and Gadja land clearance and stock numbers (which reduced the availability of traditional food resources). The Bama were outnumbered, but were nevertheless a decidedly prominent proportion of the district's population.

White settlers, therefore, had begun to come to some understanding with the Bama, and many were employed on Gadja selections. As in other areas of the Tablelands, some firm friendships arose from these interactions. The new cash crop of coffee was introduced in 1896, and the 'whole area of small acreages from Kuranda to Koah'[106] utilised Djabugay labour[107] to harvest the beans. Five years later a severe black frost destroyed most of the coffee trees, although Alf Street and J. Driscoll carried on for another twenty

2.15 *Alfred Street's coffee plantation utilised local Djabugay labour to harvest the crop.*
(Photo from *Our First Half Century*, Queensland Government, Brisbane, 1909, opposite p. 128.)

years.[108] The employment opportunities for Djabugay from Middle Crossing and Sandy Island continued well into the twentieth century.

The northern Djabugay were described by Archibald Meston as 'the old Port Douglas tribe [as well as] a few of the Mowbray River blacks [who] are camped a short distance along the beach from Port Douglas'. He explained how '[s]ome of the men and women, come daily into town and work for people who treat them fairly, and feed them well. Their old hunting and fishing sources are also available, being very little affected by the small and scattered suburban settlement'.[109]

The Queensland Government in 1888 had established the practice of distributing food to Aboriginal groups, so that they would not raid the settlers.[110] By 1896, £288, 3 shillings and 5 pence had been spent at the Barron River, Myola and Port Douglas distribution points. This amounted to 1.7 per cent of the total of £17 345, 11 shillings and 11 pence for fifty locations throughout the colony, over a fourteen-year period.[111] The government of the day was obviously not swayed by the comments of the editor of the *Cairns Argus* on 8 May 1895:

> A spectacle was witnessed on the first day of the present month—a kind of Government function, that certainly was not creditable to the authorities and should bring a blush of shame to the cheeks of every colonist. About 150 aborigines assembled in the police paddock, and the officers of peace opened a bale of blankets containing fifty, tore them in halves, and distributed them amongst the dusky natives . . . There seems to have been some qualms of conscience passing through the official mind in Brisbane

in connection with this half-blanket distribution farce, for at the very time grinning recipients were clutching their coverings a telegram came through from the capital stating that every aboriginal in the colony, except those permanently employed on stations, was to receive a whole blanket. Astounding magnanimity! We have taken from the Queensland natives no less than 428 663 360 acres of land. Out of this vast and luxuriant area about ten million acres have been sold for six and a quarter millions cash. Another three hundred millions of acres have been leased, from which the State derives an annual rental of £332,800. In return for this the Governments, past and present, have given these black-skinned, patient, uncomplaining children of the soil one whole blue blanket per year, costing perhaps five shillings each! And yet we profess to call ourselves Christians, and even set about in a spasmodic way to try and save our black brothers' souls! Can anything be more pitiful, more degrading to our boasted civilisation, more fiendishly selfish, more devilishly unjust, more indicative of British national greed?

In 1897 *The Aboriginals Protection and Restriction of the Sale of Opium Act* was passed. It came into effect on 1 January 1898. It began the long period of oppressive authoritarian control of Aboriginal people. The Act rapidly underwent

a series of alterations at the hand of politicians, the bureaucracy and the Queensland Police Force, [and] produced regulations that impinged on the Aborigine's right to marry, to live with their children, to work and control their wages, savings and property, to plead in a court of law and to travel. The Act rendered them liable to indefinite incarceration without trial and if under sixteen years of age, to flogging for minor offences committed on a reserve or mission. The regulations proscribed certain religious and cultural practices that were considered inappropriate and they also encroached on the right to own animals and even on the burial of Aboriginal dead. On missions and reserves the regulations directed that their mail be censored and the decision as to whether it was ever delivered at all to the Aborigines rested with the superintendent.[112]

It took a further eighteen years before this legislation had a profound impact on the Djabugay. In the meantime many of the Bama became fringe dwellers on the edge of European settlements,

2.16 Original caption: 'Aborigines—Kuranda, ca.1912 (natives [now] at Mona Mona Mission)' (From Queensland Parliamentary Papers, *1913.) Elders have identified Starlight Street on the far right, and other relatives are still remembered.*

(Photo courtesy of John Oxley Library.)

distraught at the loss of the living symbols of *Bulurru*, through the loss of plants and animals that were not only 'bush tucker', but also a part of the spiritual link to the *Gurra-Gurra* (ancestors).

Djabugay

3
Mission Days (1913–1962)

The first decade of the twentieth century saw a relatively amicable accommodation between the Djabugay and the white settlers in the Kuranda district. Bama were employed by local white settlers and lasting friendships were established, some of which continue to the present day.

R. B. Howard in the Annual Report of the Chief Protector of Aboriginals for the year 1912 stated: 'On reaching Kuranda, I found between 50 and 60 natives camped on the [Barron] river; they were in good health and free from alcohol and opium addiction.'[1]

The following year saw the establishment of the Seventh Day Adventist Mission twenty-odd kilometres north-west of Kuranda near Flaggy Creek (see Map 2 on page 14).[2] It was from the Djabugay word for Flaggy Creek, *munu-munu*, meaning 'crooked', that the Monamona Mission gained its name.[3] Within four months there were twelve Djabugay resident, and the reserve was described as being

> many thousands of acres of land still in the state of nature, over which they can roam at will . . . we have been able to awaken quite an interest regarding the mission in the minds of many natives scattered throughout this large district. The fact that the natives did not know us, made it difficult to approach them; and little can be done for them till their confidence is gained . . .

3.1 *This photograph of the Monamona Mission appears to have been taken between March and September 1914. Superintendent J. L. Branford (with beard) appears in the centre. The clothing worn by the Mission Bama was donated by members of the Seventh Day Adventist Church who read appeals from the missionaries for '[a]ny kind of garments for men, women, and children . . . but we would request that only sound garments be sent, especially for men, as their work is rough, and strong clothing is required to withstand the wear and tear'* (Australasian Record, *17 July 1914, first request was in the 23 February 1914 edition.*)

(Photo from the Queensland Aboriginal Protector's Report 1914; courtesy of John Oxley Library.)

[those] . . . living in the camps around the towns are all in a more or less demoralized state, being steeped in tobacco, and when they can procure it, opium, morphia, and alcohol; but not all are hopeless.[4]

It is amazing that one year before, the same group of people were described as being 'free of alcohol and opium addiction'. It would seem that the missionaries were not beyond a little fabrication, not to mention that they knew the Bama, under missionary regulations, would not be allowed to 'roam at will'. In 1914 the first Mission Superintendent, P. B. Rudge, stated that '. . . thirty natives gathered here . . . More than one-third of these are men of a very good stamp, who can do almost every kind of work we require, and have received training either on missions, stations, farms, or about town, and consider themselves civilized'.[5] Later in the same year, the second Superintendent for Monamona, J. L. Branford, wrote: 'The Mareeba Tribe are settling down nicely many of them have goten [sic] over the Morphia habit there are a few that are a little trouble

3.2 At Street Creek/Barron Falls Camp, taken before February 1916, 'when sixty-four Djabugay who the authorities described as "poor, destitute aboriginals . . . [were] removed for their own good" from Kuranda to Mona Mona'. On the left is Billy Hobbler; fifth from the left is Jimmy Snider (waistcoat and goatee beard); fifth from the right is Mary Hobbler with daughter Norah (mother of Mrs Enid Boyle), to her left is Nellie Hastie, Biddy Hobbler (in striped blouse, mother of Mrs Maggie Donohue), Topsy Courtney (in white, mother of Katie Diamond), and on the far right is Olga Street's mother. The little boy in the front on the right is Willie Newbury.

(Photo courtesy of the Historical Society of Cairns.)

yet.'[6] In response to this same letter, Chief Protector Bleakley gives an insight to the racial perspectives of the time, when he wrote to Branford:

> There is no need to register the births of full-blood children or of quadroon children whose fathers are aboriginals, but you could keep a record of your own for information.
>
> Halfcaste children of white fathers and the children of halfcaste women, except those married to or living with aboriginals should be registered as they are of value to the State on the population return under the Commonwealth per capita grant of 25/- per annum. Halfcaste women are also entitled to the

Maternity Bonus, if their husbands are at least half white or if the children are illegitimate. Applications for such bonuses should be made to the Postmaster at the nearest town where such children can be first registered.[7]

At the end of 1915 the population had reached 103.[8] This increase occurred after the removal of fifty-six Bama from Mareeba.[9] Buluwanydji Elder, the late Warren Brim, recalled:

> They got picked up at Speewah see, them Riley's family got picked up in Mareeba. The Police went down there and tell them to go up to Police Station and they give 'em blanket. When they went up, they locked 'em all up . . . old fellow know . . . Selwyn . . . 'cos his eldest brother got locked up. Went down to Djabugay camp [at Mareeba], all decided to leave that evening, run away see, and when they come down here . . . they got to Speewah . . . the Police were waiting for them.[10]

'All tribes on the frontier used runners who moved with incredible speed through the bush and in rough country were often faster than horsemen.'[11] The Djabugay also utilised runners. Elder, Selwyn Hunter has stated that we 'always had a message boy—if he didn't make his destination, didn't do his job, ran behind time',[12] so that it was felt that the runner in this instance had failed to do his job properly, and that was the reason the Bama had fallen into the Police trap.

As in other areas on the Tablelands, some white settlers[13] tried to prevent police removing local clan groups from their traditional homelands, but the power of the police and government and its bureaucracy was apparently unassailable. Licensee of Hunter's Barron Falls Hotel, Ernest Hunter, telegrammed the Hon. Theodore that 'Kuranda blacks [were] forcibly taken by contingent police [to] mona mona mission today against their will including some only signed on by protector few days ago disgraceful buiness [sic] . . .'. He commented in his follow-up letter that 'They are of great service to the inhabitants and give no trouble to the Police'.[14] Fellow Kuranda resident, M. Fitzpatrick, also sent a telegram, but to the Hon. McCormack, complaining that 'Kuranda Blacks all taken by force special contingent police two in handcuffs no notice given to employers under agreement and agreements not cancelled matter demands immediate enquiry Taken to mona mona mission Kindly attend on behalf of Kuranda people'.[15] These enquiries elicited an official

3.3 *Monamona Mission in 1916, taken from the Oak Forest Road in the old section, looking north-east with the original Bama village with locally sawn planks and roof shingles. The increase in Bama Mission numbers, with the removal of sixty-four Djabugay in February 1916 to Monamona, can be observed when contrasted with Photo 3.1. See also Map 7 for context location.*

(Photo courtesy of John Oxley Library.)

response from the Home Secretary's Office directing the Protector of Aborigines in Cairns 'to exercise his discretion in the matter of allowing any of these aboriginals who are now in employment under agreement, to remain in such employment';[16] however, it seems likely that the official intention was influenced by a report written two years earlier, which recommended the removal of 'all natives'.[17]

Elder, Warren Brim,[18] remembered how old Mrs Veivers tried to warn the Bama that the police were waiting to arrest them. Descendants of early white settlers, like George Austen Jnr, remembered his Aunt Rose Veivers of Speewah 'tearfully telling how the police on horseback used their whips when herding the Aborigines'.[19] George Austen's father as a lad in Kuranda 'had a young Aboriginal friend who taught him to catch fish under the banks of the streams, how to stay under water using reeds to catch ducks by their

3.4 *The first Girls' Dormitory at Monamona Mission in 1914. This was the old site for the mission, and was taken from old Kyber Farm Road, looking east (see Map 7). The fate of this building can be seen in the next photograph.*

(Photo from Queensland Aboriginal Protector's Report 1914, courtesy of John Oxley Library.)

feet and to use the stone axe to get honey from trees. He tried unsuccessfully to hide his young friend when the Police rounded up the Aborigines and herded them to Mona Mona Mission'.[20] This occurred in 1916, when sixty-four Djabugay, whom the authorities described as '[p]oor, destitute aboriginals [were] removed for their own good'[21] from Kuranda to Monamona. *Galgas* (spears) and *yimbis* (dilly–bags) were left at the Kuranda police

3.5 *Cyclone damage, 1919. This photograph shows the remains of the Girls' Dormitory shown in Photo 3.4.*

(Photo courtesy of Jilli Binna Museum.)

station.[22] This brought the mission population to around 167 people.[23] Many individuals or groups were forcibly removed from as far

3.6 *Flaggy Creek in flood, 1919. In the same year as the cyclone (1919), Flaggy Creek flooded and caused difficulties in transport to and from the Mission. Ironically, four years before in November 1915, Pastor Branford was decrying that the Mission was 'passing through one of the most serious droughts that has ever been known in these parts' (*Australasian Record*, *29 November 1915, p. 5). One can judge the contrast by viewing Flaggy Creek in a dry period during the 1940s; see Photo 3.16.*

(Photo courtesy of Jilli Binna Museum.)

3.7 *During the 1920s the Djabugay camp on the edge of the Mission retained members who practised traditional ways. On the left is Tommy Hobson (who probably gained his name from the white Hobson at Myola), and* Nguunba—*George Kuranda/Carroll (centre) who lived in the 'old camp'.*

(Photo courtesy of John Oxley Library.)

afield as Mossman, Port Douglas, Mt Mulligan, Ravenshoe, Chilligoe, Georgetown, Normanton, Coen and the southern Atherton Tablelands.[24]

3.8 Old Djabugay Camp, Monamona, 1917. Granny Mary Hobbler is sitting down on the right preparing guln.gay *(black pine), while Granny Annie is standing on the right (in white), next to Toby and Annie Brim (and baby Esther on hip). While second from the left, standing, is Topsy Courtney, and sitting, Middie Brim.*

(Photo courtesy of Jilli Binna Museum.)

By 1915, over 150 acres of scrub land had been cut and burnt and Rhodes grass introduced, along with maize, and eight acres cleared for vegetable gardens.[25] The Mission House and Girls' Dormitory and seven 'native' cottages, a barn and wagon shed had also been completed. Amongst other improvements the previous year, eight bridges and a road to Oaklands Railway Station (now known as Oak Forest) were constructed. The Mission was also beginning to make an income from timber-getting while at the same time investing in twenty-four bullocks. It is apparent from these activities that quite dramatic changes were starting to be wrought on the environment. The impact of increasing numbers of cattle, which had reached 160 by 1919, was not to be fully realised until the 1950s. Unfortunately for the Mission, the February cyclone of that year devastated the settlement: '. . . of the whole mission establishment, only 2 official's [sic] houses and 3 native cottages [were] left standing'[26] and all the fences were blown down and the plantation and crops were levelled. Twenty-five 'native' cottages required rebuilding. From 1914 to 1925 Pastor Branford was the Superintendent.[27] According to Elder, Flo Williams:

That's the one who used to take us away from our people when we was all young. Taken away from our custom and this tongue we can't talk—we dropped it straight off. You had to stay in the dormitory until you get married. We was going to school at that time—Branford's time, his daughter used to teach us.[28]

Since 1916 several traditional Bama camps had been located on the edge of the Mission. The Djabugay camp was located east of the Mission, but had moved to the other side, west–north–west of the Mission site by the early 1930s.[29] Elder, Enid Boyle, recalled that 'we were outside of the main Mission, separate . . . Djabugay couldn't mix in with the others. The missionaries termed them "wild people". They wouldn't allow them to mix or go into the compound'.[30] *Nguunba* (George Kuranda/Carroll) lived in the 'old camp and used to stand guard and warn "*Gadja* come now"—and we'd head out bush, and so Missionary Branford and Borgas came at night to get children for [the] dormitory. Some children didn't like to leave. My father died and I was taken . . .'[31] Elders still remember *warrma* (corroboree) and how they would participate, but by the late 1930s *warrma* in the 'old camp' was coming to an end. Dr Norman Tindale recorded in 1938 that

> in the evening we went to the native camp away from the village, where the older people still live, away from the mission atmosphere. A large crowd gathered for the corrobori [sic]. One man sings and while the women sit and thump their thighs to make hollow sounds in rythm [sic], all the rest dance, silently, or with shouting as the theme demanded. Leg-shaking dances are of first importance, and the change of tempo in keeping with the song, and sudden pauses also were important features.[32]

According to Grandma Flo Williams, the term 'king' was applied to the man who had fought many times and thereby obtained many wives. Apparently this applied to old Jackie King, the father of Peter, and father-in-law of Maggie Donohue. King Peter and Queen Maggie lived at Kyber Farm, where King Peter died in the 1950s. Queen Maggie later moved to Monamona, and later returned to live in Kuranda where she was well respected. She died at the age of ninety-one on 20 April 1995.

From 1916 through the 1920s there was another traditional camp which was made up of Muluridji and other non-Djabugay-speakers. The distinct camps with their traditional alliances meant they did not

3.9 *Jackie King was from Port Douglas way (personal communication, Elder, Flo Williams). Here he greets members of the party of J. C. Peterson (Queensland's Home Secretary) on their visit to Monamona Mission station in June 1931.*

(Photo courtesy of John Oxley Library.)

interact with one another—'Djabugay couldn't mix in with the others'.[33] The original land grant for the establishment of the mission was just under 4000 acres (1619 hectares).[34] In 1922, 318 acres were acquired to the south-east of the Mission; this became Kyber Farm. This was Reserve 598, which encompassed blocks 67 and 68.

According to a descendant of the white 'pioneers', '[b]y 1925 all the blacks of the Mowbray area had taken up residence at Mona Mona Mission Station . . .'.[35] However, in April 1934, following a medical survey by Dr Raphael Cilento,[36] five adults and two children were removed to Monamona Mission. In the intervening month between the medical examination and the removal order, two of the Four Mile Beach Camp residents had died.[37] The oldest person to be removed was *Warringinya*.[38] She had been born in 1864, and in the thirteenth year of her life in 1877, as she was crossing the threshold to womanhood, she no doubt would have been an observer of the coming of the Gadja to the coastal area that became Port Douglas. *Warringinya* lived just long enough to see herself removed from her *Bulmba*, even though Monamona was still a part of her

3.10 *Coastal Djabugay, Four Mile Beach Camp, Port Douglas, 1920.*
(Photo from *Queenslander*, 17 January 1920; photographer Keith Kennedy, courtesy of the N. H. Rex Collection.)

traditional lands. Within two months of her arrival at the Mission, in the period of *Djindjim* (dew time) of *Gurraminya* (Dry Season) *Warringinya* passed away.[39] She was quite likely relieved to be released from the burden of coming to terms with the destruction of her clan and their unique way of life.

The Mission developed relatively independently of government funding up to the period of the Second World War. Vegetables and crop growing were quite successful during this time[40] and at least five different farms operated: Bean Tree Farm, Pineapple Hill Farm, Piggy Farm, Hershy Farm and Kyber Farm. The cattle herd numbered 300 in 1931[41] and supplied 'a beast every fortnight for native rations'.[42]

The main source of income for Monamona during the 1920s and 1930s was the timber industry.[43] However, between 1927 and 1934 there was a series of complaints from the local District Secretary of the Australian Workers' Union in Cairns, the Malanda branch of the

3.11 *The sawmill in 1920 (see Map 8), where 'Mona Mona men cut timber for their homes' (personal communication, Elder, Selwyn Hunter). Note the men standing underneath the structure in order to draw the saws down when cutting the slabs. In November 1914, it was noted that '[t]he pit-saw is busy cutting out timber, and the building of the new dining-room and kitchen is going ahead'* (Australasian Record, 9 November 1914, p. 8). *The main source of income for Monamona during the 1920s and 1930s was the timber industry and by 1938, 32 000 super feet of timber was being milled.*

(Photo courtesy of John Oxley Library.)

3.12 *Harvesting the corn crop at Monamona in the 1930s.*

(Photo courtesy of Jilli Binna Museum.)

Returned Soldiers' Association and one Councillor Bartley of the Woothakata Shire Council (later the Mareeba Shire Council). The main bone of contention was that the Mission was 'operating to the detriment of white workers in the district'[44] and that 'Cairns Timber Ltd was benefitting from cheap labor [sic], not the Mission'.[45] The Mission was in fact not breaking any industrial award, and in fulfilling its contract with Cairns Timber Ltd employed three white men 'for timber felling and logging. Mission aborigines are employed as offsiders only'.[46] It is difficult to understand the niggardliness of these vexatious complaints, although no more were registered after this.

3.13 *White missionary homes at the old Mission site in the early 1930s. The garage was where Superintendent Borgas housed his vehicle. This was taken from the Oaklands (Oak Forest) road, looking south-west (see Map 7).*

(Photo courtesy of Jilli Binna Museum.)

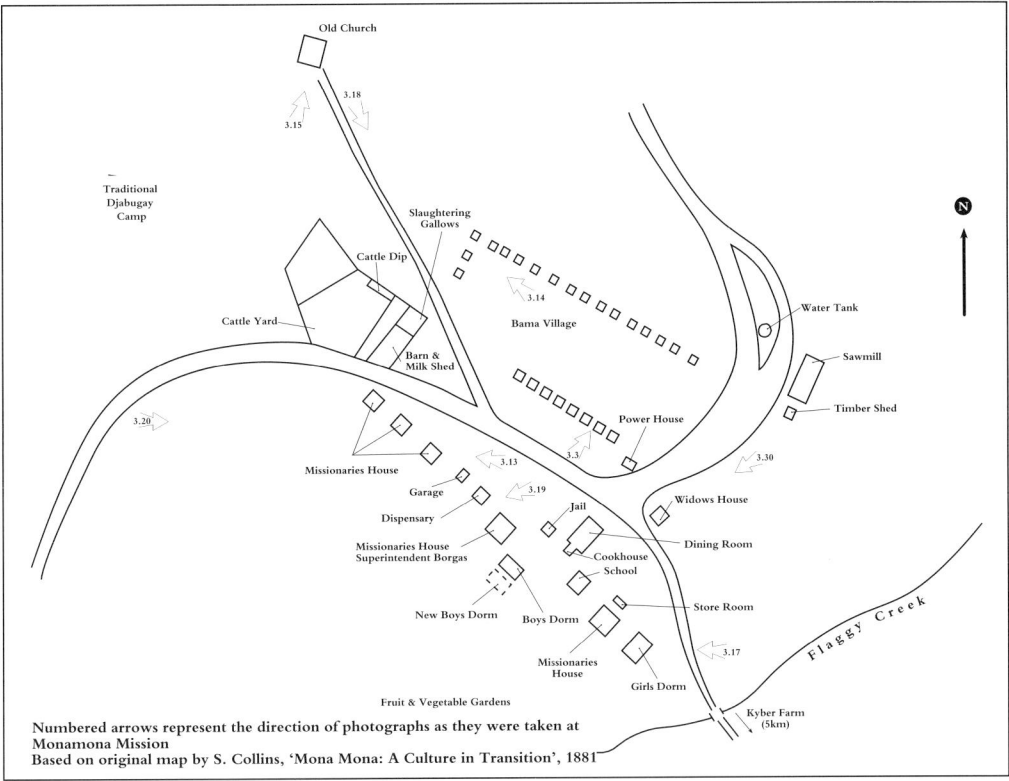

Old Church

3.18

3.15

Traditional
Djabugay
Camp

Slaughtering
Gallows

Cattle Dip

3.14

Cattle Yard

Bama Village

N

Water Tank

Sawmill

Barn &
Milk Shed

Timber Shed

Power House

3.20

3.13

Missionaries House

3.3

3.30

3.19

Garage

Widows House

Dispensary

Jail

Dining Room

Missionaries House
Superintendent Borgas

Cookhouse
School

New Boys Dorm

Store Room

Boys Dorm

3.17

Missionaries
House

Flaggy Creek

Girls Dorm

Fruit & Vegetable Gardens

Kyber Farm
(5km)

Numbered arrows represent the direction of photographs as they were taken at
Monamona Mission
Based on original map by S. Collins, 'Mona Mona: A Culture in Transition', 1881

Map 7 *Monamona Mission, 1930s*

Nevertheless, the Mission milling operation was doing so well that, by 1938, 32 000 super feet of timber was being milled.[47] The original Mission village site had gradually given way to a new site on higher ground, and to avoid fragmentation of the community the old village houses were moved. The new houses were better equipped and roomier than the former style, although quite simple by today's standards.

During this period, there were some white Australians who were raising doubts as to the wisdom of how indigenous Australians were being treated. One such person was the anthropologist, Ursula McConnel, who wrote regarding Cape York Peninsula in the August 1936 edition of *Walkabout*:

Perhaps if we were not in such a hurry to 'civilize', we might, by translating our beliefs and customs into terms more suitable to his own, encourage him to be himself, instead of, as usually happens, putting him at a disadvantage by drawing detrimental

3.14 *Old Mission Village, 1920s. One visitor in 1915 described Monamona as '[n]ineteen neat little cottages [which] house the natives, who are well cared for. The group of buildings, which consists of a large dormitory for girls, having two rooms for Brother and Sister G. Mitchell, one very large dining-room and kitchen, which serves also as the chapel, two cottages for Brethren Branford and Totenhofer, a large barn, outhouses, and milking yards, are nearly all built from the surrounding bush timber' (Australasian Record, 3 January 1916, p. 4). This photograph shows the same cottages in the 1920s, looking north-east to the wooden church (see Map 7).*

(Photo courtesy of Jilli Binna Museum.)

contrasts. The gentle art of making the other person 'feel at home' is better understood by the native in our presence than we manage in his.[48]

Over the years that followed, the way the Djabugay and fellow Bama were treated on the Mission depended very much on the temperament of the Superintendent. During Superintendent Branford's time, the government doctor was used to examine 'inmates' who had been 'troublesome'. This usually resulted in them being sent

3.15 *Monamona Church and congregation, 1920s. Saturday best for the Seventh Day Adventist Sabbath, including two Bama with slouch hats and uniform, who were members of the community Police Force.*

(Photo courtesy of Jilli Binna Museum.)

away to Palm Island[49]—an Aboriginal penitentiary.[50] The threat of being sent to Palm Island was used right up to the time the Mission closed.[51] In fact, unknown to most of the Bama, the Mission was nearly moved from Monamona to Orpheus Island,[52] in the Palm Island group. It seems the Bama were not the only people who found their Superintendent trying, as the Deputy Superintendent on Fantome Island wrote of Pastor Borgas and his companion's visit, that '[t]he gentlemen concerned are rather difficult too'.[53]

The periods from 1925 to 1931 and 1934 to 1948 saw L. A. Borgas as the Superintendent,[54] and he was responsible for severe punishments.[55] Mrs Jessie Donohue remembered that you had to 'tow the line—if troublesome, you were dealt with by caning'.[56] Another Elder recalled: 'If young people ran away, they were given a public flogging, and all the community had to see it.'[57] Family members were often forced to implement corporal punishment. Mrs Brim recalled one instance where

> the older brother had to give his younger brother a flogging. He had to lean over the table, but after five strokes, the older brother broke down and cried. This was the first punishment that touched me—I could never forget that. All us children cried and begged them not to do it.[58]

3.16 *Elder, Selwyn Hunter identified this as a baptismal service on Flaggy Creek, one Sunday afternoon in the 1940s. The ceremony began on Friday afternoon, 21 July 1916, when five 'promising' young people, 'a young married woman and four dormitory girls, were baptized . . . One feature which makes this service memorable [is] that these five young people are not only the first at the mission, but are the first Aborigines in Australia to be baptized'* (Australasian Record, *21 August 1916, p. 4). Presumably this relates to the Seventh Day Adventist Church.*

(Photo courtesy of Jilli Binna Museum.)

It was not until after Pastor Borgas left in 1948 that public flogging gradually stopped.[59] Grandad Fagan observed: 'We weren't treated like a human being, more like a dumb animal.'[60]

The housing arrangements at Monamona were strictly divided between the white missionaries and the Bama. Children were taken from their families and put in single-sex dormitories from the age of six or seven. Emma Johnston recalled:

> All the girls lived there until they got married. There were about 50 or 60 girls in the dormitory, in different sections. The teenagers would be in one part, the little ones at the other end, and the others in the middle room. There was a matron for each group of girls.[61]

3.17 Located on the old Mission site, this was the Girls' Dormitory in 1929, seen from the road to Kyber Farm, before Flaggy Creek, looking west.

(Photo courtesy of Jilli Binna Museum.)

Boys were treated in a similar manner, and contact between the boys and girls and between the children and their parents was very restricted.[62] Parents were allowed to see their children every Friday evening for ten minutes.[63] Children were punished for speaking their

3.18 Looking south-east over the Mission in the 1930s. To the left are the 'cottages' of old Mission (seen from the opposite direction in Photo 3.14). To the left and above the telegraph pole is the sawmill, while the buildings to the centre and right are white missionary houses, Dispensary, Dining Room and Girls' Dormitory. The road from Oakland (Oak Forest) comes in on the right. (See Photo 3.20 and Map 7.)

(Photo courtesy of Mrs Esme Hudson.)

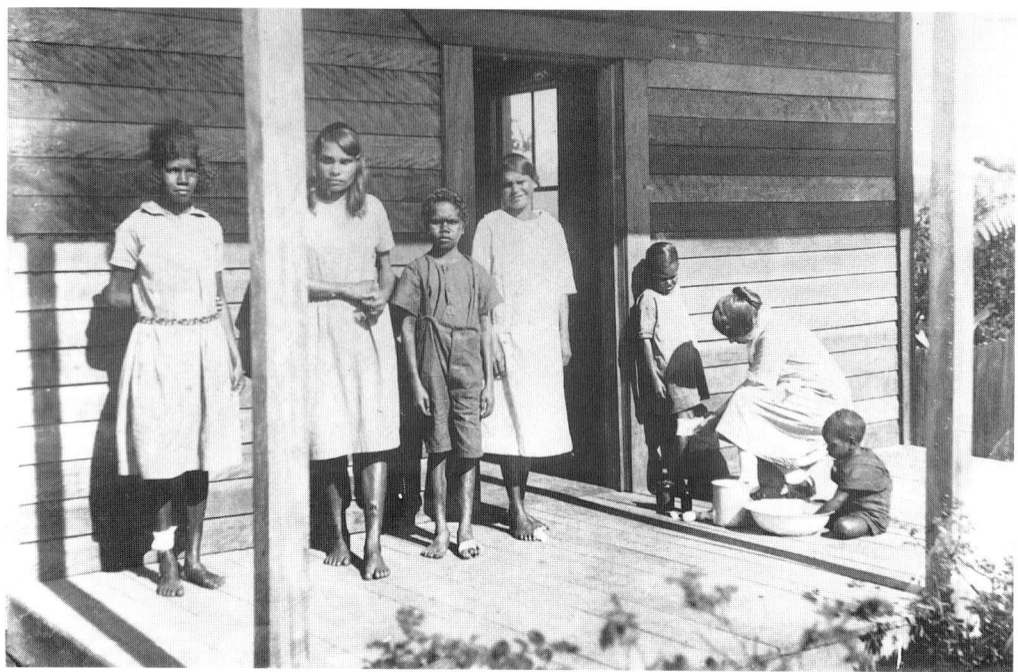

3.19 *The Dispensary was located in the south-western position of the old Mission during the 1920s and 1930s. From the left is Mavis Donald and Hazel Alpin, and next to the door is Rosie Grogan, while the white missionary helper is Pearl Branford (personal communication, Elder, Flo Williams). (See Map 7.)*

(Photo courtesy of Jilli Binna Museum.)

3.20 *First view of Monamona, looking east, from the road coming in from Oakland (Oak Forest). The row of houses seen in the middle distance were occupied by white missionary staff (see Map 8). The old village 'cottages' can still be seen, which suggests this was taken in the 1930s.*

(Photo courtesy of Jilli Binna Museum.)

own language. One can comprehend the fear with which some missionaries were held, for, even though the missionaries were in their office half a mile away, Winnie Brim's mother would whisper 'we can't teach you language—don't ask why'. Mrs Brim sadly recalls that the 'one thing I missed out on was not being allowed to learn my language'.[64] Mrs Marita Hobbler fondly remembers her grandparents as 'lovely old people who used to sneak around to the dormitory and bring the children smoked wallaby in a dilly bag because they knew the children didn't have enough to eat'.[65] Elders today still vividly recall the pain of being separated from their mothers and family.[66]

To get to the populous centre of Cairns (13 000 in 1935) from the Mission involved taking the train from Oak Forest, or making a 176-kilometre drive via Mareeba, Atherton, Yungaburra and the single-lane Gillies Highway (opened in 1926). One could take the extremely rough and precarious Bump Track to Port Douglas, but the coastal road to Cairns was not opened until 1933. The Kuranda Range Road was not opened until 1941.[67] However, it was via the Gillies that Dr Norman Tindale and Dr J. Birdsell of the Harvard/Adelaide Universities Anthropological Expedition made their way to Monamona in late August 1938. While Tindale and Birdsell's information has proven to be advantageous to current generations, it was not quite perceived in the fashion that Tindale recorded. He wrote that 'the Aborigines . . . are most willing to be measured and studied',[68] while an Elder today recalls that 'as a young chap, I thought what I was seeing and going through was very rude and rather insulting',[69] whilst others resented the indignity of being measured in their underwear.

Despite their dietary requirements being seen as deficient, Monamona received a glowing report in comparison with Yarrabah and Palm Island in early 1937.[70] Three residents were diagnosed with Hansen's Disease (leprosy) and sent to Peel Island in Moreton Bay. Another thirteen followed the next year, but only one was sent in 1939.[71] Fantome Island in the Palm Island group became an Aboriginal leprosarium in 1940 and indigenous sufferers on Peel were transferred there.[72] It might be worth noting that Hansen's Disease was considered a problem for all Queenslanders during this period,[73] although the State Government spent ten times more on each white sufferer than it did on each indigenous sufferer.[74] It was partly due to these circumstances that the Director-General of Health recommended the government's acquisition of Orpheus Island, with the intention of resettling the whole Monamona community there.[75] However, the church authorities, responding to Pastor Borgas' assessment, wrote to the Department in early 1941 stating that 'after careful consideration it is considered the site is unsatisfactory and that we are not now interested in this proposition'.[76]

Mission life was ruled by the bell:[77] it governed when to get up, when to eat, when to work, when to go to church; and like in so many other reserves, it put a stop to Bama sacred rituals such as funerals and initiations and prevented elders from passing on their language and culture. Over the years the mission changed the people's way of life. The mission lands were exploited for timber and areas were cleared for cultivation and for keeping beef and dairy cattle. The mission people gained experience in farming, forestry and the hauling and milling of timber.[78]

The coming of World War Two saw many changes to Mission life. Cairns and the rest of Cape York Peninsula were 'invaded' by American and Australian Armed Forces, with camps being established all around the Atherton Tablelands. Rowena Sheppard recalls that 'they had an airstrip in Mareeba at that time . . . there was Army and aeroplanes . . . just all over, the Mission and Mareeba'.[79] Elder, Lyn Hobbler observed:

> Before World War Two, we knew that there had been a First World War. We had never seen so many convoys of trucks—it caused a lot of excitement. When we saw black U.S. soldiers— these black people from America, in the navy, they were different people from us—they did things that white people were doing— unusual.[80]

The Mission Bama had glimpsed an insight into the potential for equality and possibly justice. It offered hope. The friendliness of the Armed Forces[81] towards the Monamona people naturally was well received, and people recalled how they 'showed Black American soldiers how to throw boomerangs and spears, as well as how to make baskets'.[82] 'When they came out, they used to go up there and buy baskets. They used to come by every Sunday to buy it. They were mad on these black kids.'[83]

It must be remembered that missionary education up to this point had been very rudimentary, and that there was no such thing as 'mass media': it was wireless or newspapers. Neither of these was very accessible to Monamona residents. The 'Missionary had a wireless and people would listen nearby, and pass on information about the war'.[84] Despite their limited access to information about the world and the war that was raging across it, the Mission Bama still made their contribution. Government authorities acknowledged that Aboriginal labour was 'instrumental in harvesting crops [on the Atherton Tableland] which were considered essential to Primary Industry'[85] and to the war effort.

An incident which many Elders recall with great amusement was the Japanese invasion of Monamona. Far North Queensland was on a war-footing, as the frontline on the Australian mainland. Parents on the Mission would frighten their children if they misbehaved, with the warning that the Japanese would kill them, somewhat akin to the role of 'quinkan' or 'debil-debil'. Near Oak Forest, just north of the Barron River, residents making their way towards the Mission noticed men in the trees by their shadows on the ground. These men were not white and looked similar to the Bama's perceptions of what Japanese looked like. The word was out—'The Japanese are coming!!'[86] 'Paddy Hasties grabbed 6 or 7 children and ran away',[87] while Mona Fagan did the same, and 'took children into the scrub and told Dora Veivers [a local white woman], who loaded a shotgun in readiness'.[88] Finally a policeman[89] came out from Kuranda and interviewed the 'invaders', only to find that they were Javanese, not Japanese. This is definitely in the 'tall tales, but true' category, and is not as unlikely as it may first appear. In 1944, the Netherlands East Indies Forces Intelligence Service 'took over The House on the Hill from ZES special units and accepted responsibility for the training of the Dutch Indonesian Service'.[90] The majority were men from Java, and their camp was located in what is now the Cairns suburb of Bungalow.[91] They were being trained to infiltrate behind enemy lines, and the '[t]raining went on day and night at the beaches and on the sea around Cairns. For special exercises they were taken to a secret training area behind Hartley's Creek, on the Cook Highway'.[92] Many times they were secretly dropped off 'back of Redlynch', and were required to find their way back to camp undetected.[93] It therefore seems quite likely that it was these Javanese, while on one of those 'secret' patrols, who were sprung by the Bama!

Despite almost thirty years of the Mission's existence, and the determination to stamp out traditional ways, some facets lingered on. Dr S. Lambert of the Western Pacific Health Service wrote in 1942, that

> on several occasions he had seen evidence of death from fear. On one case there was a startling recovery. At a Mission at Mona Mona in North Queensland were many native converts, but on the outskirts of the Mission was a group of non-converts including one Nebo, a famous witch doctor. The chief helper of the missionary was Rob, a native who had been converted. When Dr. Lambert arrived at the Mission he learned that Rob was in

distress and that the missionary wanted him examined. Dr. Lambert made the examination, and found no fever, no complaint of pain, no symptoms or signs of disease. He was impressed, however, by the obvious indications that Rob was seriously ill and extremely weak. From the missionary he learned that Rob had had a bone pointed at him by Nebo and was convinced that in consequence he must die. Thereupon Dr. Lambert and the missionary went for Nebo, threatened him sharply that his supply of food would be shut off if anything happened to Rob and that he and his people would be driven away from the Mission. At once Nebo agreed to go with them to see Rob. He leaned over Rob's bed and told the sick man that it was all a mistake, a mere joke—indeed, that he had not pointed a bone at him at all. The relief, Dr. Lambert testifies, was almost instantaneous; that evening Rob was back at work, quite happy again, and in full possession of his physical strength.[94]

However, not everyone was so lucky. According to Elder, Selwyn Hunter, at Monamona, this 'medicine man killed two mission Bama after being stopped from voodoo, one of which was an Aboriginal policeman'.[95] It was during the latter stages of the 1940s that the traditional camp of the Djabugay declined, and by the early 1950s had disappeared altogether. Nevertheless, all through the time of the Mission, an important traditional nut-cracking site had continued to be used in secret, and the knowledge of its use and location was kept from the missionaries.[96] There are many *gundjinarr* (pitted rock slabs) found at this important site, where *gurrndu* (Kuranda quandong) were cracked with a *gundji* (nut-cracking stone).[97] Not far from *Yiwurra* (Black Bean) Crossing on Troughton Creek, this ancestral camping site was a Bama secret for over seventy years.

Unfortunately, 1946 was a drought year which saw forty per cent of Monamona's cattle herd die,[98] along with the associated difficulties that water shortage causes to farming. This prompted the construction of a 35 000-gallon concrete water tank the following year and they began the process of installing an irrigation system.[99] The Superintendent wrote that they had 'begun an extensive agricultural progress' with the expansion of goat numbers: 'Not only are they good from the milk and meat point of view, but as we house them in sheds with a grating for a floor we collect much valuable manure for the vegetable gardens.'[100] It was in this year that Monamona formed its

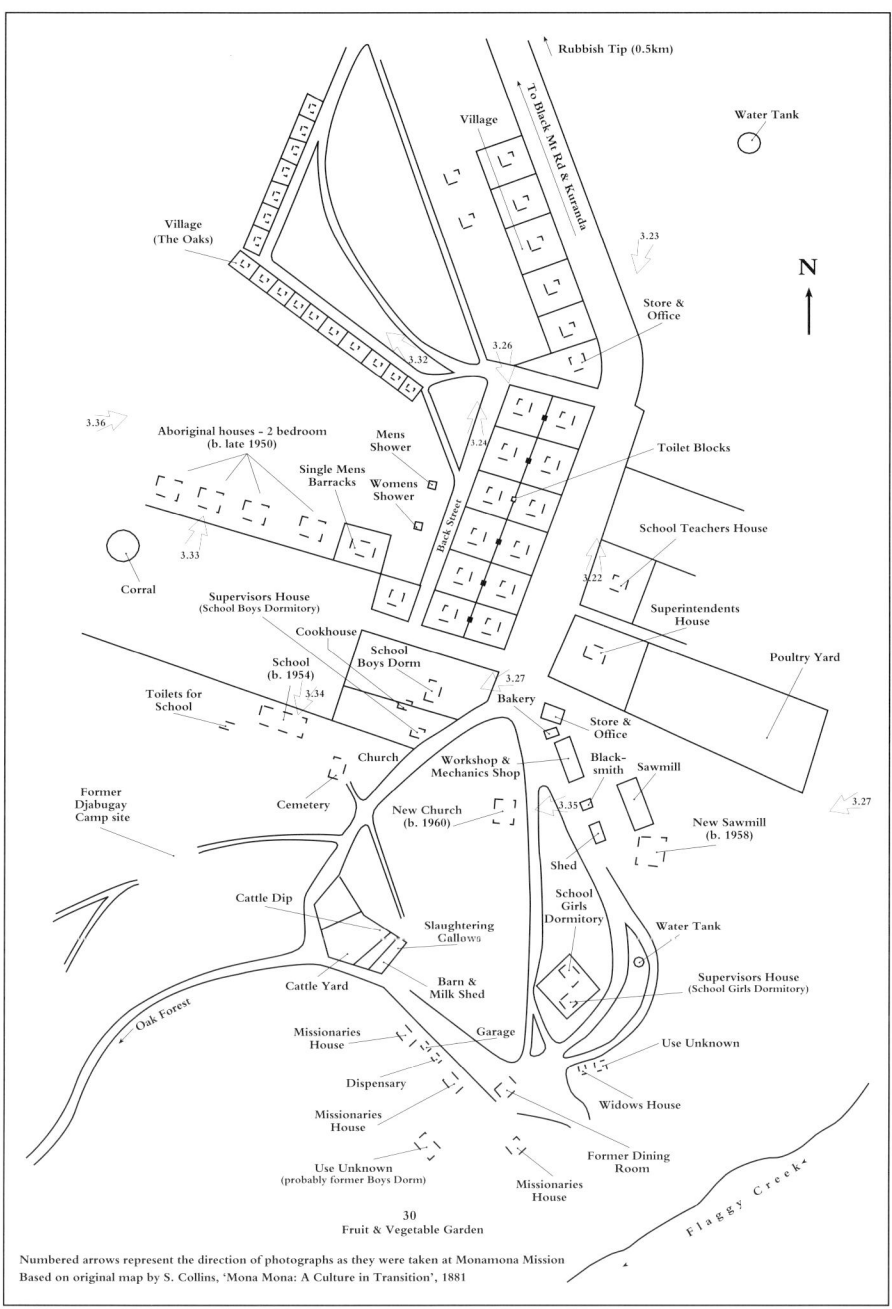

Rubbish Tip (0.5km)

Village

To Black Mt Rd & Kuranda

Water Tank

Village
(The Oaks)

3.23

N

Store &
Office

3.26

3.32

3.36

Aboriginal houses - 2 bedroom
(b. late 1950)

Mens
Shower

Toilet Blocks

Single Mens
Barracks

Womens
Shower

School Teachers House

Back Street

3.24

3.33

School Boys Dormitory)

3.22

Corral

Superintendents
House

Supervisors House
(School Boys Dormitory)

Cookhouse

Poultry Yard

School
Boys Dorm

School
(b. 1954)

Toilets for
School

3.34

3.27

Bakery

Store &
Office

Church

Blacksmith

Sawmill

Former
Djabugay
Camp site

Cemetery

Workshop &
Mechanics Shop

New Church
(b. 1960)

3.35

New Sawmill
(b. 1958)

3.27

Shed

School
Girls
Dormitory

Cattle Dip

Slaughtering
Gallows

Water Tank

Supervisors House
(School Girls Dormitory)

Oak Forest

Cattle Yard

Barn &
Milk Shed

Garage

Use Unknown

Missionaries
House

Widows House

Dispensary

Missionaries
House

Former Dining
Room

Use Unknown
(probably former Boys Dorm)

Missionaries
House

Flaggy Creek

30
Fruit & Vegetable Garden

Numbered arrows represent the direction of photographs as they were taken at Monamona Mission
Based on original map by S. Collins, 'Mona Mona: A Culture in Transition', 1881

Map 8 *Monamona Mission, 1952*

3.21 *The new location for Bama houses on the Mission in the 1950s. Looking north-north-east, with* Bunda Bugal *(Black Mountain) dominating the skyline. This appears to have been taken from the school teacher's residence. (See Map 8.)*

(Photo courtesy of Mrs Carol Estree.)

choir and brass band, which was to be such a source of pride and entertainment for the Mission Bama.

Meanwhile, whilst many Bama were adapting to Mission life, a small group of Djabugay were living close to a traditional lifestyle in the Freshwater valley, where they were able to maintain the Stories and language. This they were able to do, as they were not subject to Mission rules. This was to be the saviour, in many ways, of traditional knowledge of the Djabugay. These people were the descendants of Buttercup and Tambo Banning who lived and married on their traditional lands encompassed by Andrew Banning's selection. Buttercup and her mother, Minnie, had escaped the Speewah massacre, probably in mid-1890.

Certainly post-World War Two Monamona contrasts quite sharply with the period before 1940. Elder, Lyn Hobbler recalls that there were great changes for the better, especially with transport, as the 'missionaries got army transport cheap . . . fancy an Aboriginal driving a truck—the kids were impressed'.[101] In mid-1945, the newly-wed couple, Pat and Gwen Blanch, arrived. He worked at the sawmill

3.22 *The housing arrangements at Monamona were strictly divided between the white missionaries and the Bama. Looking south, on the thoroughfare out to Black Mountain Road, around 1948.*

(Photo from *Queensland Parliamentary Papers*, 1949, Vol. 3, p. 36, courtesy of Mrs Carol Estree.)

and she as a nurse. Mr Blanch's time saw 'more freedom of speech, and he understood what we was going through'.[102] The firm foundation of love and friendship between Monamona residents and the Blanch family was laid during the period 1945 to 1951.[103] Mrs Winnie Brim fondly recalls her first job as house-girl to Mrs Blanch, and how she helped the future Mrs Brim by making her wedding dress for her. The warmth of the relationship between the Blanches and the Bama community was to be demonstrated a decade later when as Pastor, Pat Blanch returned to help his friends in the Kuranda district.

The 1950s were still a time when wages earned by 'inmates' were banked for the worker and access was restricted. Permission from the Superintendent was required, along with justifiable reasons for what the money was to be used for. Such restrictions were a part of everyday life for the descendants of the Bama. In 1951 the Superintendent, Pastor G. Peacock, stated that 'We are gradually but surely proving that agriculture will prove the main stay [sic] of the Mission'.[104] But seven years later Superintendent Litster reported that

3.23 *From the Back Street of Monamona, looking north in the 1950s (personal communication, Elder, Selwyn Hunter). (See Map 8.)*

(Photo courtesy of Jilli Binna Museum.)

3.24 *Timber logging on Black Mountain Road.*

(Photo courtesy of Jilli Binna Museum.)

3.25 *Looking south-east, with Back Street running along the housing fence-line to the right. The main thoroughfare is to the left, running between No. 2 Settlement and Superintendent's (top left) and the school teachers' residence. The dark and light tones of the houses symbolically confirms the division between staff and 'inmates'. (See Map 8.)*

(Photo courtesy of Jilli Binna Museum.)

'Our efforts to produce payable vegetable crops have been disheartening, due to the poor nature of the soil'.[105]

The first half of the decade saw a rapid turn-over of Superintendents, with a subsequent decline in the standard of administration of the Mission. Some five Superintendents held the position over four years and five months, from March 1952 to August 1956.[106] It was during this period that health and sanitary conditions deteriorated, enabling a serious problem with hookworm and parasites to develop.[107] The problem peaked in 1959, but by 1962 the number of hookworm sufferers had been reduced to six.[108]

The superintendency of Norman Ferris, from 1956 to 1958, is not remembered fondly. He is considered *warray*—'no good': 'Every Tuesday of second week endowment paid; we had six children, never told how much we getting—no money, went almost three months without payment.'[109] Whether the financially strained coffers of the Mission were the recipients of the child endowment payments, it is

3.26 *Front view of the Little Boys' Dormitory for under-ten-year-olds, 1950s. The dining room is in the background on the left. This was taken looking east, opposite the store and office. (See Map 8.)*

(Photo courtesy of Jilli Binna Museum.)

not too difficult to judge, as a precedent had already been set in 1941 when £1500 of these payments were incorporated into Mission funds.[110] On one occasion Mr Steven Fagan approached Ferris to find out how much he had in his account, and he was threatened with being sent to Palm Island if he did not stop asking questions. This was a regular threat used against the Bama. Officially, Ferris was reprimanded on several occasions,[111] and in relation to his first breach 'It was made plain to him

3.27 *Monamona Brass Band in Coondoo Street, Kuranda, on Anzac Day, 1950. The band was formed in 1946 and was a source of much pride and entertainment for the Mission Bama.*

(Photo courtesy of Mrs Carol Estree.)

3.28 *This 1936 D50 International truck was used only on rare occasions, and was used in 1951 to take the Monamona Brass Band and their instruments to play at an Innisfail Festival (personal communication, Elder, Selwyn Hunter).*

(Photo courtesy of Jilli Binna Museum.)

3.29 *During the 1950s, Sunday evangelist meetings were held at the Cairns Palace Picture Theatre (now Geo Pickers, on Mulgrave Road), and the Monamona Choir sang regularly at these gatherings (personal communication, Elder, Selwyn Hunter).*

(Photo courtesy of John Oxley Library.)

3.30 *Singing Mission Bama, 1930s. Elder, Flo Williams recalls that this group used to sing for visiting government officials (like the Chief Protector of Aborigines, William O'Leary). Somewhat ironically, one of the main songs was 'God Bless Our Lovely Morning Land Australia'. The shed behind the group was the sewing machine house (at one stage the widows' house). Immediately behind the shed is the large dining room (see Map 7); next to that on the right (out of sight) was the jail. The Superintendent's house is just visible to the right.*

(Photo courtesy of Mrs Carol Estree.)

that you cannot punish a person by cutting out his foodstuffs'.[112] Apparently, Ferris was also a keen punter. Shortly afterwards Ferris was killed when his vehicle was struck by another just outside Townsville.[113] Another Elder remembers 'Pastor Norman Ferris got good money out of cattle—won prizes, but we never knew what happened to the money'.[114] The Church and State seemed to have shied away from answering questions in this regard, although it seems likely that monies made were used to pay off Mission debts already incurred.

By October 1958 'there were 318 native persons on the books but the actual population was closer to 260 of whom over 100 were children of school and pre-school age'.[115] More emphasis was placed on education and the dormitories were phased out; however, the pernicious control of the people remained in the form of the 'permit system'. This required any Aboriginal who was not officially exempted from 'the Act' to seek permission and obtain a 'ticket of leave' to visit Kuranda or any-where outside the Mission. Elder, Finlay Grogan, describes the process:

> During the week we weren't allowed . . . to go anywhere [without] the permission of the Mission. But if we come to Kuranda for the day, then you get permission. You gotta be back there—little ticket you know, you go into Kuranda for a day—couple of day, then when your time's up, you gotta go back home. If you're not home that certain day, you're in trouble. You might have to go to jail for a couple of days.[116]

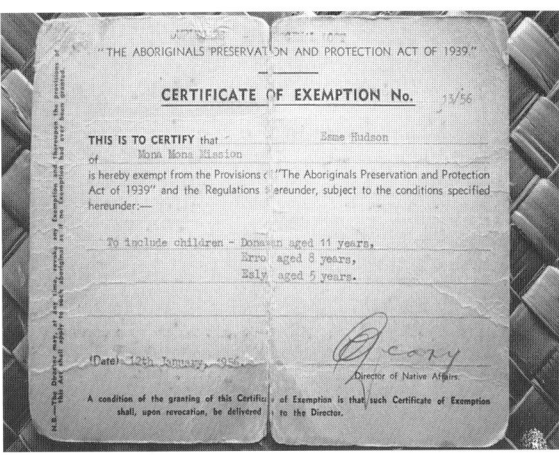

3.31 *Mrs Esme Hudson's Exemption Certificate issued on 12 January 1956. Note on the left of the document: 'N.B.- The Director may, at any time, revoke any Exemption and thereupon the provisions of this Act* [The Aboriginals Preservation and Protection Acts, 1939–1946] *shall apply to such aboriginals as if no Exemption had ever been granted.' Several Elders quietly expressed the need to keep their Exemption card, just in case they were re-introduced!*

(Courtesy of Mrs Esme Hudson.)

Throughout the twentieth century, it had always been the police who had been responsible for enforcing removals and chasing up absconders from the permit system. It is therefore not surprising that 'Aborigines did, and still do, resist police authority, not simply, as many white people believe, from a sense of bloody-mindedness, but from frustration emanating at least in part, from historical injustice'.[117] Despite this, many ex-Mission Bama fondly remember the feeling of community where 'We were all one, a happy family',[118] and decry many of the problems relating to alcohol, drugs and selfishness that have developed amongst their children and grandchildren's genera-tion. Elder, Finlay Grogan, summed it up when he said that 'we used to be "jack of all trades"—to see young people today makes us sad'.[119]

A part of folklore which happens to be true was the scandal in 1960, when one of the Mission lads ran off with the daughter of two white staff members. Apparently she was keen to leave, and one Friday night pushed the lad into taking her on his borrowed horse

3.32 *The Mission houses relocated to 'The Oaks' village site (see Map 8). Grandad Selwyn Hunter took this photograph in the 1950s. The baby is Loretta Baker, the horse 'Old Brownie', and Martha Hunter is washing clothes in the background (in front of the horse). Note the primitive standard of housing.*

(Photo courtesy of Jilli Binna Museum.)

to Oak Forest. They moved on to camp above the rapids between Oak Forest and Koah and spent the day in unmarried bliss. The next day they made their way to Oak Forest where a policeman picked them up. The girl's parents were distressed at her disappearance and felt the lad should have brought her back, but were accepting of his reticence for the escapade in the first place. They did not want to press charges, but Superintendent Litster did, and the lad spent nine months in Stuart Creek Jail, before being let out early on good behaviour. He was 'more upset with the Superintendent as [he] should have left it to the father'.[120] The young man had not realised the girl had been interested in him, but the way the Bama interpreted this incident was that 'If you go with a dark man, it's wrong, but it's alright for a whiteman to go with a dark woman'.[121] This is an insight which also highlights the hypocrisy behind the denigration of the so-called 'halfcastes' for their mixed heritage, and yet fails to acknowledge the role played by white men in creating the situation in the first place!

The Mission continued to cut timber on its own land and to train timber workers as well as encouraging 'employable natives' to accept work outside, as this experience was considered 'a big step on the road to assimilation'.[122] Mrs Winnie Brim remembers that the 'missionaries encouraged people to leave, if work was available, without really telling them why'.[123] To what degree the knowledge that the State Government planned to build a dam on Flaggy Creek in the not-too-distant future influenced the desire for the promotion of the Federal Government's policy of 'assimilation' is not too difficult to gauge.[124] Monamona Mission was becoming a financial burden on the Church[125] as well as on the State,[126] and no doubt the signs of technological development suggested that it was a convenient solution to the Church and State's respective problems.

Authorities were therefore quite gratified that they could report that an 'increasing number of natives . . . are working outside the Mission on the Railway, Forestry, and at sawmills'.[127] In the 1963 *Queensland Parliamentary Papers* for 1962, nary a mention was made of this Mission which had existed for fifty years. It is rather sad that 'the missionaries never even came and said goodbye'[128] to the Bama when the Mission closed. Officially Monamona had ceased as an entity. 'We were told,' Mrs Jessie Donohue recalls, 'that they were going to flood Monamona—we felt helpless . . . had to go, otherwise they send the police—to take us

3.33 This house was occupied by Sarah and Henry Hunter. Four of these two-bedroom houses were built in the late 1950s and were located west of Back Street, Monamona. (See Map 8.)

(Photo courtesy of AIATSIS and the After 200 Years Photographic Project.)

3.34 Completed in 1954, the school and recreation hall had been completely removed from the site six years later.

(Photo courtesy of Jilli Binna Museum.)

3.35 *Completed in 1960, the new Seventh Day Adventist church was removed from the Mission two years later, leaving only the concrete and brick steps.*

(Photo courtesy of Jilli Binna Museum.)

to Yarrabah, we had no choice.'[129] Mrs Rowena Sheppard recalls reasons given why they were forced to leave: '. . . irrigation . . . the Government said they were going to put a big dam out the Mission and it was going to be covered with water and everybody had to leave . . . it was just a big sham'[130]—an understandable interpretation considering that the dam has never been built.

Many Elders 'felt that we were pushed out of the Mission; the change came overnight, and we didn't know the value of money'.[131]

Similarly, there was resentment about the Church's selling of Mission fixtures, such as the sawmill and Kyber Farm. The ex-residents received nothing from monies made in this respect. In March 1963, the Co-ordinator General's Department compensated the Seventh Day Adventist Church with £23 000, and the Department of Native Affairs with £10 000.[132] Further criticism has been levelled at Church and State authorities for not aiding the Bama in gaining some form of employment. Some local white residents came to the aid of several Bama families, not only in finding accommodation, but also employment. Some hard-working men from the defunct Mission found employment in the Department of Forestry, or working for the railways, or in private timber-milling companies.

The main area of mission land was redesignated from the status of 'Aboriginal Reserve' to 'Electrical Works Reserve, R1219'.[133] All buildings were either removed to villages along the railway line or sold off to surrounding farms. During October 1962[134] Mission Bama moved to Koah, Oak Forest, Kowrowa, Mantaka (the original Djabugay name was *Mandjaga* (personal communication, Elder, Florence Williams, 18 September 1998), although white 'settlers' used to refer to it as Welcome Pocket), Kuranda or Mareeba. However, it must be remembered that 'it was the government that broke the Mission, not the people, but the Bama were expected to pay for the houses to be moved to their new locations'.[135] Despite the passage of time, strong ties to the Mission area have remained for the former Monamona residents and the traditional Djabugay owners.

3.36 Monamona Aboriginal Reserve was officially closed from 1 January 1963, and all that remained standing was the water tank and fencing.

(Photo courtesy of Jilli Binna Museum.)

Certainly all the hard work and commitment that the Bama and missionaries alike put into the vision that was Monamona Mission appeared to have been in vain. The role of the Government and Church authorities is reminiscent of James Boswell's observations of another player, that they 'fed you with a continual renovation of hope, to end in a constant succession of disappointment'.[136]

Djabugay

4

This Side of the Railway Tracks (1963–1997)

Monamona Aboriginal Reserve was officially closed on 1 January 1963.[1] The control of Aboriginal people in the State of Queensland was such that the Bama felt the helplessness of not being able to combat their autocratic eviction, along with a sense of betrayal by the authorities concerned. In the closing days of the Mission the attitude of residents was 'Well you took the place from us you look after us'.[2] The residents did not want to move, and wanted to retain 'their identity as a body'.[3]

Despite the inability of both Church and State Authorities to see the Bama perspective in relation to compensation (in fact it was not even a consideration in official correspondence), the Seventh Day Adventist Church Authorities had no 'intention of deserting the people'.[4] They had even suggested an 'early walk-out' from administering the Mission, which the Department of Native Affairs considered 'most inopportune'.[5] This possibly accounts for the government's largesse to the Church regarding financial compensation. While a Church representative could state that 'we are firmly convinced that the step we are taking in handing the Mission over to the Government is in the best interests of the native community as it will hasten the integration of many families with the white community and bestir many to get out and work, thereby proving they are able to fend for themselves', it was still felt necessary to give 'pastoral care that the

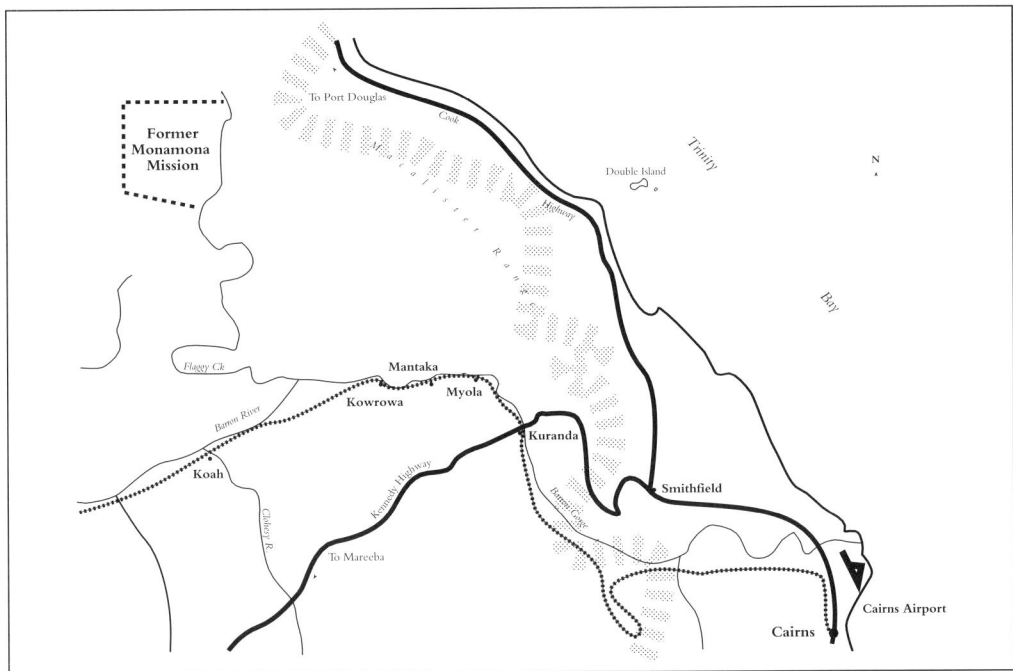

Map 9 *Kuranda District, 1998*

natives deserve and need'.[6] Thus it was that Pastor Pat Blanch, a former member of staff at Monamona Mission was directed 'to act as Welfare Officer to offer counsel, as well as spiritual help'.[7] Pastor Blanch helped a great many people, those in the Church, and those who were not. 'He had a love for all people and was well and highly respected',[8] and worked tirelessly for the community. On one occasion he mortgaged his house in Sydney in order to help Wilfred Levers buy his own house;[9] an act which Mr Levers still recalls with gratitude and admiration for the faith Pastor Blanch had in him. In a similar fashion, despite official obduracy regarding indigenous Australians, local white people in the Kuranda district maintained good relations with the Bama. Barry Hunter Snr recalled that

> older white people would socialise with older Bama. My father used to always talk about the Veivers and Austen mob, as they used to work for them. There was a fond relationship between the old whites and old Bama.[10]

It is worth noting that many Djabugay took their surnames from their first white employer; for example, Hunter, Donohue, and

4.1 *This was the standard of accommodation for the Redlynch Djabugay in 1967.*

(Photo from *Northerner*, 7 April 1967.)

Banning. It is a positive reflection on the Kuranda community today that racial accord is such that there is a lot less racial tension than in other rural centres.

Over ninety per cent of non-Aboriginal Australians voted 'yes' to amending two sections of the Constitution in a national referendum in May 1967. The Federal Government could now assume responsibility for Aboriginal people in the States, which it failed to do until the Whitlam Government in 1972.[11] Prior to the second amendment, Aboriginal Australians were not counted as Australian citizens. The Bama in the Kuranda district either had little knowledge of this referendum or knew about it but did not fully understand its ramifications. Although it was acknowledged that the 'Referendum . . . [was] . . . when Aboriginal people were free to vote, allowed to go into hotels and to drive, along with other people'.[12]

In the late 1960s, hippies discovered Kuranda, and their relaxed lifestyle meant that they 'accepted the Bama as they were and socialised with them'.[13] It was with these growing relationships that the different components of Kuranda society began the process of better understanding between black and white. Queensland was still operating under a bastardised version of the 1897 Act,[14] and reserves were still tightly controlled by the Director of the Department of Aboriginal and Islander Affairs, Patrick Killoran. By early 1967, the Bama at Redlynch were living in shocking conditions.[15] The Assemblies of God owned a building close to the camp. But when it became clear that the church was interested only in saving the souls of the Bama, and not in making its land available to improve living conditions, the church was told, in no uncertain manner, that its visits were not welcome. Apparently some of the local cane farmers literally got 'up-in-arms' about the camp at Redlynch. One concerned white helper was threatened on two occasions with shotguns by cane farmers.[16] In another instance, it is alleged that armed farmers surrounded a cane paddock ready to shoot a Redlynch Bama, falsely accused of interfering with a local white primary school girl. The police had to be called in to defuse the situation. The *Northerner* demonstrated a more fair-minded attitude when it wrote:

> Certainly the existence of 'the camp' at Redlynch is a blot on the Northern conscience . . . No more so, perhaps, than any of a dozen other such settlements within an easy day's drive of Cairns, but one that might, conceivably, be a place to start giving a depressed section of the community some help. The cane farmers, after all, weren't backward in coming forward when they thought they had a case.[17]

An Aboriginal teacher and black activist, the late Mick Miller, recalled: 'In those days . . . [white] people were so used to bullying Aboriginal people and getting away with it. They bullied the Redlynch people . . . with their standover tactics, and because the Redlynch people didn't have anybody at that time to stand up for them, or support them, they went along with them.'[18] Meanwhile,

> when the Cairns Progress Association protested against the appalling plight of families on the Aboriginal reserve who lacked cooking, washing or sleeping facilities, Killoran justified inaction by claiming the occupants were 'transients' and 'squatters'. He directed police to evict them, ordering 'the entire "fringe" community to be cleared up' and families relocated in town. Like so many others, this group refused to move, citing 'a tribal affiliation for this area', a connection confirmed by the federal DAA [Department of Aboriginal Affairs] officer who declared that the community had long occupied the area, maintaining tribal and sacred links. Similar processes of attrition covering several decades are well documented on official files for communities at Normanton, Croydon and Birdsville, to name just a few.[19]

The Redlynch mob merely wanted some dry shelter during *Gurrabana* (Wet Season), and the Cairns Progress Association managed to supply them with seven caravans. Four wet seasons later the caravans had virtually fallen to pieces. Eventually in 1976, the Djabugay of Redlynch obtained, with the help of the housing society Woompera-Muralug, two blocks of land at Caravonica and one at Harvey Road, Redlynch, where houses were built. The latter was occupied by Buttercup Banning and her son Gilpin.[20]

Efforts by Djabugay, fellow Bama and concerned white advisers to improve their living conditions were continually thwarted by the very department whose existence was ostensibly for the benefit of indigenous Queenslanders. It has been said that:

> In an aggressive campaign to dismember rural enclaves, Killoran missed few opportunities to exert pressure. A Seventh Day Adventist worker assisting local Aboriginal families at Kuranda was informed that 'a condition of payment of further subsidy' was his agreement to inculcate 'right assimilation attitudes'. You must 'conform to departmental policies of assimilation', he was told, and 'encourage movement of former Mona Mona mission residents now in the Kuranda area to those centres where work opportunities presents'.[21] Although direct federal housing funds were available for local Aboriginal communities who formed the prerequisite co-operatives, this information was not passed on by state departmental officials keen to disperse groups to available employment. Killoran also rebuffed those councils and welfare associations seeking to assist local groups in this process.

Neither would the state sanction long-term leases on reserved land, thus precluding Aboriginal access to the federal Aboriginal Enterprises Capital Fund set up to boost vocational or commercial projects. Reserved lands, declared Killoran, were held 'generally' for the benefit of all Aborigines and would not be allocated to specific-purpose groups. Where file evidence exists on the granting of a few special leases, these were stipulated as only short term, 'thereby ensuring that areas are not "tied up" by lease unduly long whilst perhaps remaining undeveloped'.[22]

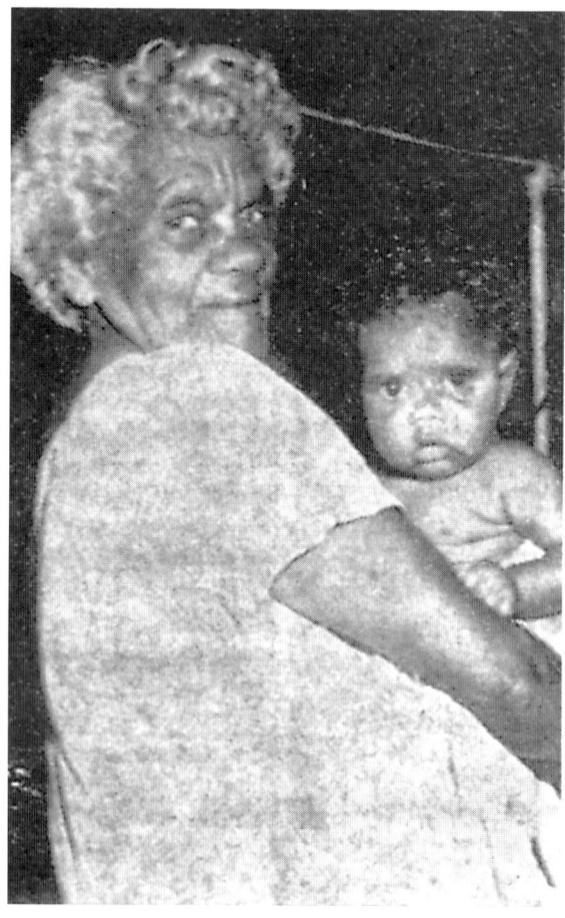

4.2 Buttercup Banning nursing her grand-daughter Nancy at Redlynch in 1967. 'Buttercup' was named after one of the Veivers' milking cows at Speewah (personal communication, Elder, Selwyn Hunter).

(Photo from *Northerner*, 7 April 1967.)

Nevertheless, the Bama, under the auspices of the founding member and first chairman, Mr Lyn Hobbler, established the Ngoonbi (pronounced 'Noon-bye') Housing Co-Operative Society in 1975.[23] This was a very important development as it gave more confidence to Bama participants, as well as developing their skills at participating in meetings; it certainly was 'a big head start'![24] Ngoonbi was established as a Co-Operative Society Limited, especially to obtain and manage housing in the Kuranda village area, and is still in operation today serving the Bama of the district. On 23 August 1979, the State Government re-gazetted the former Monamona reserve, from 'Electrical Works Reserve' to 'Departmental and Official Purposes Reserve', 'under the control of the Under Secretary of the Department of Community Services [the successor of DAIA] as trustees'.[25] This occurred without informing or consulting with the former residents of Monamona.

It was not until 1984 that Queensland finally saw the demise of the remnants of the dreaded Act, which had so invidiously controlled their lives in various guises over the previous eighty-seven years. Although the Djabugay had not lived on the Mission since 1962, any interaction with the Bjelke-Petersen government was still dictated by the Act and the entrenched bureaucracy that implemented it. Steven Fagan was employed by a private contractor after the Mission closed, but like many other Bama, was paid via the government, that is, the employer paid wages to the Department, who then allowed only a portion to be accessed by the worker. In Mr Fagan's case, it took two years for him finally to get paid direct.[26]

Many ex-'inmates' had leased blocks of land at Kuranda, Mantaka, Kowrowa and Koah (all near Kuranda, along the Barron River), on which were moved houses, purchased by them from the Mission. These settlements are all south, or this side of the railway tracks, running from Kuranda to Mareeba, parallel to *Bana Wuruu* or middle Barron River. From the 1960s until December 1988, when the local train service ended, the Bama used to catch the rail motor as it stopped along the line picking up and dropping off passengers. This was their main mode of transport. To go shopping, to go to school or to go to work, the Bama planned their day around the timetable of the railway. The Seventh Day Adventist Church which had run the Mission, also leased an eleven-acre block at Top Kowrowa (portion 360), which they surrendered to the Lands Department in 1975. The Queensland Department of Aboriginal and Island Affairs (DAIA) was then made trustee of this block.

4.3 *Warren and Winnie Brim and their children at their home at Mantaka in 1986.*

(Photo courtesy of AIATSIS and the After 200 Years Photographic Project.)

At one stage a rudimentary water supply was provided by the Mareeba Shire Council and DAIA. It comprised an external tap for each house. For this, there was an annual fee, plus coin-in-the-slot meters. Residents recall that for ten cents, they got about 2 gallons (9 litres) of water; as Rhonda Brim lamented: 'That wasn't water, that was teardrops!' The pumps were damaged by floods. The pump motors then sat in the Council yards and the people carried water in buckets from the Barron River.

Some of the leaseholders owed rent to the Lands Department and some also owed rates to the Mareeba Shire Council. Late in 1979, at a gathering at the Seventh Day Adventist Hall in Kuranda, many of these leaseholders signed papers surrendering their leases to the Lands Department. Many later complained that they had been unsure exactly what they signed.[27] Forfeiture of the leases was gazetted in January and April 1980. The DAIA was made Trustee of this land.

Although DAIA accepted control of the land, it had not accepted responsibility for the appalling conditions under which the people were forced to live. There were three or four families living in some of these crumbling houses, without water or power. It was not until late 1981, when rumours started to the effect that housing would be built and people moved to it from their ex-leasehold blocks, that the people discovered that they no longer legally owned their land and houses.

In response to these rumours, and the discovery of their loss of leases, a meeting was held in January 1982. At that meeting, the DAIA representative promised that the people would be consulted on the design of the houses to be built, when provisional plans were drawn up. The houses were to be built on the eleven-acre block at Top Kowrowa. The Department also promised that no one would be moved from Mantaka, Koah and Bottom Kowrowa. No consultation at all took place. The first the people saw were two articles in the *Cairns Post*, dated 6 and 8 July 1986.[28] Work had started on the site by 19 July, with tenders accepted for a two-duplex, two-triplex development around a central car park.

A meeting was held on that same Monday, at which it was decided to hold a bigger meeting on the site on Wednesday, 21 July 1986, to see the plans and express opinions on the design. It was from the builder on the site that the people first saw the plans. They had expected high-set separate houses, not barrack-style housing. Speakers pointed out that the design would make health and social problems worse, not better. They were angry and disappointed, and some were too afraid to say anything!

Many Djabugay spoke of their experiences on Mona Mona, which they still regarded as their home, which was lost without a fight, and expressed their determination to hold onto what little they had left. They voiced their fears that this housing development was the beginning of a modern-day mission-cum-ghetto, to which they would be moved, thus leaving Mantaka, Koah and Bottom Kowrowa open for real estate development. Speakers had no faith in DAIA promises that no one would be moved. They had just seen one promise broken; why not others? They decided the Department could find out about the meeting the same way they did about their housing—in the *Cairns Post*.

The building went ahead anyway.

In 1986, residents of Mantaka lobbied the then Queensland Department of Northern Development and Community Services, which had supplanted DAIA. They confronted Minister Katter with their poor living conditions. The Chairman of Shelter North Queensland, Mr Bill Baird, stated publicly that

4.4 *Mr Cecil Brim's home at Mantaka in 1986.*

(Photo courtesy of AIATSIS and the After 200 Years Photographic Project.)

[u]p until recently water had to be carried from the Barron River. Now one outside tap per house has been installed. There is no drainage.

The children are forced to suffer illnesses and infections a great deal of their lives due to the intolerable and overcrowded conditions. Their schooling is also neglected through these illnesses and lack of space.

There is no electricity at Mantaka and cooking is done by wood stoves. The houses are in such a state of disrepair, accident and fire risks are high . . . to describe the living conditions . . . as deplorable would be an understatement. An atrocity is being committed against the people of Mantaka through the failure of our community to recognise the poverty in which these Australians are forced to exist.[29]

This culminated in a demonstration and occupation of Katter's Northern Development Office at Virginia House and later the Department of Community Services Offices, both then in Abbott Street, Cairns. Katter was out of town, but later met with residents

4.5 *Esther Snider with two of her nieces, at the Hunters' house at Mantaka in 1986.*
(Photo courtesy of AIATSIS and the After 200 Years Photographic Project.)

on 10 April 1986, and stated that the Government did not have the money to build any houses. Mantaka residents quizzed him, and then

4.6 *Esther and Tasman Snider's 'home' at Mantaka in 1986. Mr Snider is standing on the top steps with his grandson, Leroy Diamond.*

(Photo courtesy of AIATSIS and the After 200 Years Photographic Project.)

asked for title to the land. He reportedly said he 'couldn't see any problem'.[30] The residents took this as a tentative agreement. On the strength of that, federal funding for housing was obtained from the then federal departments of the Australian Development Corporation and the Department of Aboriginal Affairs, but when it was not used after eighteen months because of inaction on the part of the Department of Community Services in returning the land, the funding returned to the Federal Treasury. However, the initial willingness to consider transferring tenure of the land was not maintained. The Mantaka people then reluctantly agreed to rental housing from the Department. By March 1987, no houses had been built, in spite of more promises to do so. By late 1987, four houses were under construction. In the first week of March 1988, the remaining shanty houses were demolished without consultation, or adequate notice. Martha Brim recalled that when the new houses were being built 'they knocked the old houses down, and for four or five months we had to live down by the river, behind the old railway station, under canvas. It rained for a month while we were camping'.[31]

There was another meeting and the Department agreed to hire caravans and annexes, while the Mantaka people waited for the completion of the construction of the houses. Nevertheless, this required the residents to live in unpleasant camping conditions. Despite wanting ownership of the land, the Djabugay residents of Mantaka, Kowrowa and Koah have until recently been required to pay rent and did not have security of tenure. Stoves, water tanks and the old iron and floorboards from the remains of the houses disappeared without any reference to the original owners—to this day, the Mantaka people do not know what happened to the material which they could have so readily utilised.

The year 1987 saw the establishment of the Tjapukai Dance Theatre,[32] at the instigation of Don and Judy Freeman, along with a young Kuranda Bama, David Hudson, which launched the Djabugay on the road to international recognition. Employment opportunities and the recognition of the value of Djabugay cultural heritage has contributed to a resurgence of pride in the community. The Freemans' vision to put on a small play for visitors required consultation with the Elders, not only for permission, but also to teach the young men the traditional aspects of *warrma* (dance). The young Djabugay men, who had not grown up knowing *warrma*, quickly realised that the traditional movements came quite naturally. It was initially difficult to find young men who were prepared to perform in front of visitors, as there was a great deal of shyness and 'shame'. However, a number of young musicians who called themselves 'The Mantaka Band', and who played a local Aboriginal style of rock and reggae, stepped forward for the challenge. The Dance Theatre flourished in Kuranda and won international recognition which enabled them to work in with Skyrail and establish themselves in a bigger and better complex at Caravonica. The move saw a change in name to the Tjapukai Aboriginal Cultural Park.

Bina, Michael Quinn, a British anthropologist/linguist living in Kuranda, approached a number of Elders who spoke Djabugay and began the process of studying and recording *Ngirrma* (language). They began teaching the language at the Kuranda State School and then at Smithfield State High School. For *Wanyarra*, Roy Banning, Djabugay was his first language and it created great joy in him to be able to share his language and his country with young Djabugay. Together with *Galgam*, Ashley Coleman, a talented musician with a strong attachment to traditional indigenous music, along with *Bina*'s creative language games, they brought the learning experience alive for the *bibunbay* (children). This trio made up the core of the Djabugay Language School which has preserved and re-invigorated Djabugay *Ngirrma*. Smithfield State High School was one of the first schools in Queensland to teach Aboriginal and Torres Strait Islander Studies when the Board of Senior Secondary School Studies trialled the syllabus in 1996. Kuranda State High School begins teaching it in 1999. *Bina, Wanyarra* and *Galgam* were chosen to transmit Djabugay culture to the students. Young Aboriginal students from the Kuranda district had to get up early each morning (around 6.00 a.m.) to travel to Smithfield State High School to obtain a secondary education, until 1998 when Kuranda obtained its first high school on Myola Road.

It would appear that over the years the Bama have been set up to fail. Rosalind Kidd gives an insight as to how this occurred:

> The Aboriginal department in Queensland has operated since its inception as a closed, secretive and highly defensive agency of government. Remarkably, only three men held the position of chief administrator between 1914 and 1986,[33] exercising almost total control over the lives of many thousands of Aboriginal Queenslanders, regulating freedom of movement, place of residence, employment, private savings and spending, marriage, adoptions and family cohesion.
>
> Until the 1950s Aboriginal administration was largely run as a personal fiefdom. With the influx of federal funding and the accession of Killoran in the 1960s, however, Aboriginal affairs in Queensland was increasingly politicised as policies were articulated in the media and in parliament. By the late 1970s and 1980s Aboriginal affairs became a matter of state, rather than departmental, resolution. Killoran's close ideological affinity with premier Joh Bjelke-Petersen cemented a unified anti-federal stance as they rebuffed what they perceived were strategies to usurp state sovereignty and dictate state policies, particularly in issues such as land rights, self-management, and award rates.[34]

The despair and hopelessness of the Bama's situation, which no doubt directly or indirectly impacted upon their mental well-being, may possibly be gauged by the incredibly high number of deaths between 1989 and 1992. Pastor Frank Gory of the Kuranda Seventh Day Adventists presided over ninety funerals during this three-year period.[35]

By the early 1990s, Mabo and legislation being framed and

acknowledgement of the rights of traditional owners made people with traditional links (in this instance, the Djabugay) more assertive. This brought the community closer together. They now had rights and responsibilities and could influence authority within the community. Previously this tended to be directed by those with an historical link to the area.[36]

The 1990s saw some dramatic symbolic changes. The Aboriginal and Torres Strait Islanders Commission (ATSIC) was formed from the Federal Department of Aboriginal Affairs and the Aboriginal Development Commission, and is now run by and for indigenous Australians. The Mona Mona Corporation was formed and began work on rebuilding the old Mission site as a farm and home for the Bama. Prior to this, umpteen attempts had been made over the years since 1962 by ex-Monamona people to gain access to the former Mission lands, but 'there is evidence that all attempts by ex-residents to lease or purchase at the former [Mission] site were blocked by the department [of Aboriginal and Islander Affairs]'.[37] The Bjelke-Petersen government's Deed-of-Grant-in-Trust (DOGIT) legislation[38] was in any event of no assistance to Aboriginal people who lived on Special Reserves. The introduction of the Queensland *Land Act* in 1991 was the first legislation in the State that allowed the transfer or 'hand-over' of land to specified Aboriginal people with traditional, historical or economic connection. '[I]t might be thought that this was a generous gesture by the government towards traditional Aboriginals. In fact, it was a response from the State designed to head off anticipated federal legislation promised by the Hawke federal Labor government, with a view to keeping control of land administration in the State.'[39] Nevertheless, it was very important pyschologically for Aboriginal people who have both an historical and traditional association with the land in the Kuranda district, as they felt it gave security in relation to Aboriginal reserve lands and the old Mission site. It was felt that this was a confirmation of land rights, whether it actually was or not. However, the *Land Act* spurred Bama to want to take more responsibility and control of their lives. This encouraged the Kowrowa community to form the Kowrowa Aboriginal Community Association, and Mantaka to re-invigorate the Mantaka 'Shanty' Aboriginal Corporation.

The following year saw the Australian High Court Mabo decision recognise indigenous land rights. It 'quashed the notion of "terra nullius", which had long justified the dispossession of Aborigines by asserting the land was desert and unoccupied'.[40] This acknowledgement thrilled the Djabugay and fellow Bama, who at long last felt that they would see justice done. The then Labor Queensland Minister of Aboriginal Affairs, Anne Warner, visited Mona Mona, and promised to return Mona Mona land to the Mona Mona people. Up to December 1998 this promise had not been fulfilled.

However, a positive development that came out of this visit was the formation of the Djabugay Tribal Aboriginal Corporation on 7 July 1992, with Gerald Hobbler as the first Chairman. It became very active in representing traditional interests relating to cultural heritage matters and land to the various government departments. It provided a representative body for the area's traditional people, particularly in relation to language and the Djabugay Land and Natural Resource Management Office. Similarly it provided a focus whereby traditional owners gained acknowledgement of their traditional links to their *Bulmba* and enabled the recording of sacred and significant sites to be achieved. The Corporation was particularly interested in resolving the ownership disputes regarding the lands of the former Mona Mona reserve. It was proposed that ownership of Mona Mona should be invested in the traditional people to allow for everyone, both historical and traditional.

Meanwhile the Mabo decision, which recognised Native Title in 1992, was considered '[t]oo deadly . . . it's just another mechanism that we have to use to get our land back'.[41] During 1992, the people of Mona Mona and the Djabugay Corporation began to address many important issues affecting the community and their rights and responsibilities as indigenous Australians. Their course of action culminated in the establishment of the Djabugay Ranger, Land and Natural Resource Management Agency. From the initial goal settings and early efforts the Djabugay Ranger Agency now has rangers with qualifications as graduates, with diplomas of Aboriginal and Torres Strait Islander Natural and Cultural Management. The Ranger Agency has been instrumental in planning and implementing, in conjunction with Elders, initiatives at *Bunda Dibandji* (Bare Hill), as well as other key management issues associated with the Barron Gorge National Park, and Skyrail.

The advent of the Skyrail development and the new Tjapukai Cultural Park at the bottom of the range has led to a recognition that '[n]ow we seem to be more co-operative, a whole new era, it's no longer a matter of them and us'. As Rhonda Duffin from the Djabugay Corporation explains, 'by finding common ground, working together for everyone's benefit, it's a "win–win" situation, and

4.7 *The former Liberal Member of the Legislative Assembly for Barron River, Lyn Warwick (left), officiating at the Handback to Joy Hudson and Coralie Wason of the Kowrowa Land Trust, at Ngoonbi Farm on Monday, 15 December 1997.*

(Photo by T. Bottoms.)

4.8 *Lyn Hobbler, Djabugay and Community Elder, speaking at the Handback, with Rhonda Brim (Mantaka 'Shanty' Aboriginal Corporation and Mantaka Land Trust) looking on.*

(Photo by T. Bottoms.)

97

4.9 Guginy *(Flying Fox)—Wally Brim, and the vision of* warrma *for the Handback.* (Photo by T. Bottoms.)

4.10 *Inland Djabugay Country. Looking north across the corridor of valleys and streams that make up part of the traditional lands of the Djabugay.* Bunda Bugal *(Black Mountain) is in the middle distance, ten km north-west of Mona Mona. The head of Rifle Creek is located between* Bunda Bugal *and the coastal range (*Bunda Bundarra—*Macalister Range), seen on the horizon to the right of the mountain. The Mowbray River flows through to the coast about ten km to the north-east of Black Mountain.*

(Photo by T. Bottoms.)

4.11 *Coastal Djabugay Country. The coastal plain of* Bana Bidagarra *(Barron River) flows from the Barron Gorge on the left (near the foot of Glacier Rock) to its mouth, out of the picture on the right. The current Smithfield nestles at the foot of* Bunda Bundarra *(Macalister Range), near the centre of the photograph. Above the range at this point, one can just discern the tip of* Bunda Bugal *(Black Mountain). Off the coast to the right, one can just make out* Wangal Djungay *(Double Island). On the far left, the mouth of the Barron Gorge is located, below Glacier Rock.*

(Photo by T. Bottoms.)

4.12 *Handback* warrma. Ganibarra *(Dingo)—Duane Donohue*, Didjirr–didjirr *(Willy Wagtail)—Glen Williams Jnr (Slim) and* Gindan *(Moon)—Joe Snider Performing* warrma *(dance) for the Handback.*

(Photo by T. Bottoms.)

4.13 Gindan *(Moon)*—*Joe Snider imbued with the spirit of* warrma.

(Photo by T. Bottoms.)

4.14 *Sharing.* Garna *(Black Cockatoo)*— *'Cookie' (Martha) Brim, showing visitors to the Tjapukai Cultural Park the intricacies of plant use for medicine and food.*

(Photo by T. Bottoms.)

4.15 *'For future generations.' Elder, Grandad Selwyn Hunter showing future generations how to make a freshwater fish trap.*

(Photo by T. Bottoms.)

nobody loses out this way'.[42] Unfortunately, however, many white people doing business with the Djabugay see it as being too difficult for the Bama, and that they know best and always want to control ventures, without giving any credibility to the Djabugay and their ability to organise and run ventures for and on behalf of their own community.

However, in October 1997, the Queensland Government 'agreed to sign over three reserves of land [at Koah, Top and Bottom Kowrowa and Mantaka] and place them in the hands of Aboriginal trusts'.[43] Five weeks later:

> The Premier [Rob Borbidge, Leader of the Queensland National Party] officially handed over four small parcels of housing land . . . 'I hope it answers in some quarters the senseless criticism that I am a racist redneck,' he said. Ms [Rhonda] Brim was more concerned about finally winning back the land than Mr Borbidge's reputation . . . 'Now we have got the land back we are just elated,' Ms Brim said. 'It is for the benefit of our children's children to carry on . . . It is a start and hopefully we will get more land back that is rightfully ours.' The land has been made available under the Goss Labor government's Aboriginal Land Act, which set up a basis for land claims and the transfer of certain categories of land to indigenous people.[44]

Thus on 1 December Bottom Kowrowa was officially handed back, and on 10 December 1997, the Governor of Queensland, His Excellency Major-General Peter Arnison, signed the documents necessary to effect the transfer of the other small parcels of land. When Mantaka and Top Kowrowa were officially returned on 15 December 1997 the Djabugay communities celebrated with great enthusiasm, including performances by the Tjapukai Dancers. Koah is expected to obtain its title deeds in March 1999, due to problems associated with easement access by fellow landowners.[45]

Nevertheless, the question of what happens to the former Mona Mona lands has still not been settled. It is now thirty-five years since the residents of Mona Mona were ejected, in order to build a dam that has not been built. The continued vacillation by the State Government bureaucracy over this same period to stop the Djabugay and historical Bama from returning to settle at Mona Mona, along with the rapid expansion of Cairns and increased water demands, suggests that 'the powers that be' are not going to give up on the project. What then of the legitimate land rights of the Djabugay for their traditional *Bulmba*, now so minutely encompassed by the original Mission boundaries?

One cannot help but agree with Bachelard that

> it is beyond question that if we create a future in which we remain wilfully blind to the rights of indigenous Australians, we condemn ourselves to repeat the sins of the past.
>
> Aboriginal Australians have already suffered massively at the hands of colonists, and the actions of subsequent governments have done little to reduce that suffering. Many Aborigines enjoy few of the services and utilities that other Australians take for granted. White Australia has removed their access to land and to a traditional way of living. For many it has removed their Dreaming, and failed to replace it, or even recognise the magnitude of the dispossession.
>
> Native title . . . and the High Court had shown the way. A lucky few indigenous people, it seemed, could escape the fate of dispossession and hand-outs because the English law had finally recognised what they had known all along—they had a law of their own, and it entitled them to land in this country.
>
> The Wik decision expanded that promise to a whole new realm. It allowed Aboriginal access to the vast rangelands of Australia, the pastoral holdings which are at the centre of the white myths of pioneering, mateship and triumph in adversity. It challenged the lawmakers to attempt, in good faith, to find a new way to define how two peoples could coexist on the land, it challenged pastoralists to embrace those who coexisted with them, and it challenged the public and businesses of Australia to be patient while these changes were made.
>
> If any of these groups, for reasons of greed, selfishness or political expediency, refuse to take up the challenges, our nation is diminished.
>
> We are in grave danger of that outcome.[46]

Over 120 years has passed since the Gadja invaded Djabugay *Bulmba,* and much sorrow and tragedy has been experienced by the Bama, but the heritage of a people, including an irrepressible sense of humour, which extends thousands of years into the past, could not, and would not, be ignored—they have survived! Along with fellow indigenous Australians, the Djabugay know that it is no longer a matter of if, but when, the broader Australian community recognises the original inhabitants and their specific cultural identity and links to their traditional lands, so that we can all come to terms with who and what we are, as Australians.[47] The dawning of the twenty-first century promises a more cohesive, and enlightened nation than has previously been seen, on this the oldest continent in the world. It is indeed a time when the Djabugay can look with confidence to the future and say that we are 'Proud to be Aborigine'.

Djabugay

Afterword

I arrived in North Queensland in September 1965, and in 1966 began teaching Australian history at the recently opened Townsville University College.

I immediately realised that the tropical north was different in many ways to the temperate south. The climate, vegetation, the light, the colours of the landscape were all quite distinctive. So too was the history of European settlement: it began much later than in the south. Hobart and Sydney were mature cities by the time that Townsville or Cairns were founded. Even in the 1960s the northern cities had an air of impermanence, as though the Australian colonists were still sojourners in a land that they hadn't fully adjusted to. Most people one met had only recently arrived in the north or were about to leave.

Another distinctive feature of the north was its multi-cultural and multi-racial history. The Aboriginal population along the tropical coast had been high in the era before the arrival of Europeans, with population densities greater than in many other parts of the continent. Northern tribes appear to have avoided the small-pox epidemics which decimated the southern contemporaries twice during the period 1788–1830.

When settlers arrived they came from many sources—from the southern colonies, direct from Britain, from the islands of Melanesia, from southern China and from Japan. For many years the conventional wisdom was that it was impossible for 'white' people to flourish in the tropics.

Under the influence of the White Australia Policy the Melanesian labourers were deported in 1906 and restricted immigration condemned Asian communities to a slow inexorable decline. But Aborigines and Torres Strait Islanders confounded the confident expectations of early twentieth century racists that they would 'die out', condemned by the iron laws of evolution.

Aborigines and Islanders were an unmistakable presence in North Queensland as I discovered thirty years ago. They had been moving into Townsville and Cairns throughout the 1960s as stockmen were forced off stations (because they were required to pay award wages), and as restrictions on movement were removed from residents of remote settlements and missions.

But while indigenous Australians were an everyday presence, they had gone missing from the history I was required to teach my students. In 1959 a leading historian told a gathering of his professional colleagues that one of the most distinctive features of local historiography was that in Australia it was not necessary to pay much attention to the Aborigines who were only noticed in a melancholy anthropological footnote.

This was almost literally true of the book which had been set by the University of Queensland for the course I was to teach—*Australia: A Social and Political History* (Angus & Robertson, Sydney, 1955) edited by Professor Gordon Greenwood. The Aborigines were only mentioned three times and then only in passing. They did not appear in the index. How could one teach North Queensland students about the history of their own society while using such a book?

But by the late 1960s Australia was changing. The Referendum of 1967 was a symbolic event of great significance. It was overwhelmingly carried in the major urban centres in the north. By 1970 new histories of settler–indigenous relations were appearing on bookshop shelves. Within ten years the trickle of new historiography had become a flood which helped to carry away old attitudes, to establish patterns of behaviour and belief.

So successful was the new history that conservative Australians began to worry that the ground was shifting beneath their feet. Concern turned to alarm when the judges of the High Court took up the cause and in the Mabo and Wik cases introduced sweeping changes to both history and jurisprudence. The term 'black-arm band' was coined to denigrate the new history which was condemned by Coalition politicians, corporate leaders and conservative commentators.

The Reconciliation Movement turned its attention to history, insisting that without a telling of the truth there could be neither regret nor forgiveness. Truth-telling and reconciliation were important on the national scale but they were also significant at the local level.

National stories left out too much detail, they generalised too broadly and overlooked significant variations. Reconciliation had to take place district by district if it was ever to succeed. In the process, local stories had to be told, secrets uncovered, old grievances aired, ancient prejudices exposed to view.

Local history is, then, critical for reconciliation. This is why *Djabugay Country* by Timothy Bottoms is such a welcome addition to the history of both North Queensland and of settler–indigenous relations. Timothy has worked with the local people, has heard their stories and knows the country in question. There is a foreword by the Djabugay elders who explain that the book introduces to the whole of Australia 'how we as Aboriginals experienced and remembered those early days' when governments 'did not realise how much suffering was put upon Aboriginal people'. In words that are heard in indigenous communities all around the country the elders ask: 'What does it take to acknowledge the truth of our history, and the impact it has had on us?'

The Djabugay story is distinctive just as the Djabugay country is different. As modern tourists know, the Cairns–Port Douglas hinterland is a place of heavy rain, dense tropical rainforest, towering mountains and plunging waterfalls. Settlement came late to the far north. The pioneers were usually not pastoralists driving flocks and herds before them, but loggers and miners rushing in their hundreds to the alluvial goldfields in the interior.

Djabugay country knew the killing times and Bottoms refers to several remembered sites of massacre. But some settlers established good relations with the local clans who often worked for small farmers. The dreaded and destructive Native Police Force lacked its characteristic skill at destruction, the terrain severely hampering the mobility of mounted troopers. By the 1880s public opinion in both Australia and overseas had curbed the Force's propensity to massacre and mayhem.

The Djabugay experienced the repression of the protectionist era after 1897, and several generations grew up in the dormitories of the

Seventh Day Adventist mission at Monamona where they were punished if they spoke their own language. For a long time, however, groups and individuals lived outside the mission, combining traditional hunter-gathering with casual labour for the small farmers.

So when the mission closed in the 1960s and the whole mechanism of protection was gradually dismantled, the Djabugay set about creating the conditions for their survival as a people. They had several advantages: they were still living on or near their own country and despite a century of European endeavour much of the land remained more or less as it had been before colonisation. The richness of the country for both hunter-gatherer and farmers meant that the Djabugay were better nourished over several generations than mission inmates and fringe dwellers in many other parts of the country.

Even so the Djabugay renaissance is a story for all of Australia to celebrate. The language has been retrieved and is now being taught in local primary and secondary schools. In 1987 the Tjapukai Dance theatre was established at Kuranda just as Cairns experienced a great increase in local and international tourism. The timing was exquisite. More recently the large and impressive Tjapukai Cultural Park has opened at the foot of the mountain range on the road from Cairns to Kuranda and to Port Douglas. It has become one of the most important tourist attractions in the whole of North Queensland.

Timothy Bottoms tells his story well and illustrates it with many photos. It is a local story about a comparatively small district in Far North Queensland and about the Djabugay people who have lived there for many thousands of years. It is a local story but it is one that all Australians should become familiar with.

Henry Reynolds
January 1999

Djabugay

Notes

CHAPTER 1 *JOURNEYS OF THE GURRA-GURRA (ANCESTORS)*

1. R. M. W. Dixon, W. S. Ramson & M. Thomas, *Aboriginal Words*, Oxford University Press, Melbourne, 1990, p. 2.
2. B. J. Blake, *Australian Aboriginal Languages*, UQP, St Lucia, 1991, p. 6.
3. T. Bottoms, *The Bama People of the Rainforest*, Gadja Enterprises, Cairns, 1992; south to north—Dyirbal-speakers, Yidiny & Djabugay-speakers, Kuku Yalanji, Guugu Yimithirr.
4. N. Horsfall, 'Living in Rainforest', PhD, James Cook University, Townsville, 1987. However, the date is for the site, but not necessarily for the earliest occupation of rainforest. Dr Horsfall states elsewhere that 'there is no reason to suppose that Aboriginal people have not lived in the region for most of those 40,000 or more years', in N. J. Goudberg, M. Bonell & D. Benzaken (Eds), *Tropical Rainforest Research in Australia,* James Cook University, Townsville, May 1990.
5. B. David, 'Nurrabullgin: Preliminary results from a pre-37,000 year old rockshelter, North Queensland', *Archaeology in Oceania*, 1993, 18(1), pp. 50–54. Assessments at Mt Mulligan, N.Q.
6. J. Flood, *The Riches of Ancient Australia*, UQP, St Lucia, 1990, p. 128.
7. C. Jones, 'Pollen find may rewrite prehistory', *Weekend Australian*, 20–21 June 1992: 'A palynologist, or pollen expert, Dr Kershaw believes he has found signs of human disturbance in rainforest pollen patterns in a drill core from the edge of the continental shelf 80 km east of Cairns.'
8. U. H. McConnel, 'The Rainbow-Serpent in North Queensland', *Oceania*,

Vol. 1, No. 3, 1930, pp. 348–49; 'in the heroic age . . . away out beyond Green Island at a place called Wuranyaman, which in those days was all land . . .' U. H. McConnel, 'Inspiration and Design in Aboriginal Art', *Art in Australia*, 15 May 1935, p. 52. There are other Stories of a flood recalled by Aboriginal Australia. South of the present Townsville, James Morrill, who lived with the Bindal/Juru people for seventeen years until 1863, 'related one such story when he told of the great flood which had been witnessed by their ancestors . . .', B. Breslin, 'Prologue', *The James Morrill Story*, unpublished manuscript, p. 2.

9. J. Sutherland (Ed.), *Valuing Cultures*, Key Issue Paper No. 3, AGPS, Canberra, 1994, p. 25.

10. According to Elders, Marita and Lyn Hobbler, they referred to themselves as 'Djibanydji', not Buluwanydji. Personal communication, 21 September 1998.

11. R. Banning & M. Quinn, *Djabugay Ngirrma Gulu*, Cairns, 1989, pp. viii–ix; T. Bottoms, 'Djarrugan—The Last of the Nesting', MA(Qual) Thesis, James Cook University, Cairns, 1990, pp. 11–45; D. Seaton, 'The Initiation Ceremony of the Tjapukai Tribe', *North Queensland Naturalist*, Vol. 26, No. 118, 1 September 1957.

12. R. M. Dixon, *A Grammar of Yidiny*, Melbourne, 1977, p. 6; K. Hale, 'TYAPUKAY' in P. Sutton (Ed.), *Languages of Cape York Peninsula,* AIAS, Canberra, 1976, p. 236.

13. U. H. McConnel, 'A Moon Legend From the Bloomfield River, North Queensland', *Oceania*, Vol. 2, No. 1, 1931, p. 24. An excellent coverage is given by M. Quinn, *Bama Nganydjin—Our People*, DTAC, Cairns, 1995.

14. T. Bottoms, *Yirrganydji Cultural and Historical Trail: A Short Walk on the Wild Side*, Cairns, 1993, p. 10.

15. R. Banning, M. Quinn & F. McLeod, *Bulurru Storywater*, Cairns, 1990, p. vi.

16. Ibid.; *Nyuwarri* was Queen Maggie Donohue's Djabugay name.

17. P. C. Griffin, *Yarraburra, Myths, Legends and Rock Paintings of the Yarrabah Aboriginal Reserve*, The Humanist Press (AIAS), Canberra, 1967, p. 30.

18. M. Quinn, 'Magic and Sorcery', lecture to the Djabugay Rangers, 17 March 1994.

19. U. H. McConnel, 'The Rainbow-Serpent in North Queensland', *Oceania*, Vol. 1, No. 3, 1930, pp. 348–49.

20. R. Wood, Appendix 5 in D. Rivett (Co-Ordinator), *Port Douglas and Environs Planning Study*, Prepared for the Dept of the Premier, Economic & Trade Development, Environment Science and Services, Cairns, January, 1992, Chapter 3, p. 6.

21. P. C. Griffin, *Yarraburra*, p. 30.

22. W. E. Roth, *North Queensland Ethnography*, Bulletin 14 (1910), pp. 18–19.

23. Ibid., p. 19.

24. Guginy,Wanyarra & Bina, *Buda:dji Miya-Miya-Djada*, Cairns, 1991, p. 42.

25. P. C. Griffin, *Yarraburra*, p. 30.

26. R. M. W. Dixon, *Words of Our Country*, UQP, St Lucia, 1991, pp. 28–32. Dick Moses told the Story in Yidiny, where carpet snake is *Wungul*.

27. Ibid., p. 11.

28. Ibid., p. 10.

29. R. M. W. Dixon, *Words*, pp. 32–41, P. C. Griffin, *Yarraburra*, pp. 18–23.

30. R. Banning & M. Quinn, *Bulurru Storywater*, Cairns, 1990, pp. 29–34; see also P. C. Griffin, *Yarraburra*, pp. 17–18.

31. W. F. Willmott & P. J. Stephenson, *Rocks and Landscapes of the Cairns District*, Qld Dept of Mines, Brisbane, 1989, p. 21; see also J. Flood, *Archaeology of the Dreamtime*, Collins, Sydney, 1989, pp. 189–95 (Chapter 14, 'Rising Seas and Change'): 'When the sea was rising most quickly, it could, within one generation, have drowned a strip of land over a hundred kilometres wide, which would greatly reduce a coastal tribe's territory. All over the world the event seems to be commemorated in legends about a great flood, and in Australia the stories are so detailed and specific that there can be no doubt that they recall events thousands of years ago.', pp. 189–90.

32. P. C. Griffin, *Yarraburra*, p. 23.

33. D. Seaton, 'A Legend of Durran Dae (Dream Time)', *North Queensland Naturalist*, Vol. XX, No. 101, 1 June 1952, pp. 18–19. See in contrast to this, P. C. Griffin, *Yarraburra*, pp. 26–29.

34. T. Bottoms, 'Djarrugan—The Last of the Nesting', p. 57.

35. P. C. Griffin, *Yarraburra*, p. 23.

36. D. Seaton, 'A Legend of Durran Dae (Dream Time)'.

37. 'Damarri is the mountain at Redlynch, visible from the Freshwater Hotel. The cheeks of his buttocks face upwards. He has one full right leg. His left leg is bitten off and appears as that', letter from Kelvin Hill to author dated 17 July 1990.

38. Personal communication, Djabugay Elders.

39. R. M. W. Dixon, *Words of Our Country*, UQP, St Lucia, 1991, p. 112.

40. The Bama appear to have names for sections of river (relating to their clan territory), but not for the whole watercourse.

41. Personal communication, Mrs Enid Boyle, 7 June 1995.

42. T. Bottoms, 'Djarrugan—The Last of the Nesting', Chapter 3.

43. T. Bottoms, 'Djarrugan—The Last of the Nesting', pp. 92–142. See also Chart One, p. 94.

44. The Dry Season was the period to obtain minya [edible meat—like wallabies etc.]; it runs approximately from August to early December.

45. K. Lumholtz, *Among Cannibals*, 1889, ANUP, Canberra, reprinted 1980, p. 265.

46. R. L. Sharp, 'Tribes and Totemism in North East Australia', *Oceania,* Vol. 9, 1938/9, p. 255.

47. R. M. Dixon, *A Grammar of Yidiny*, p. 9.

48. J. V. Mulligan, *Queensland Votes and Proceedings*, May 1876, p. 399.

49. Personal communication with the late Mr Warren Brim; see also T. Bottoms, 'Djarrugan—The Last of the Nesting', pp. 28–29.

50. C. Anderson, *The Political and Economic Basis of Kuku-Yalanji Social History*, p. 114.

51. W. E. H. Stanner, 'On Aboriginal Religion', *Oceania*, Vol. XXXIII, No. 4, June 1963, p. 153: '(i) The ruling stratum, the older men, enforced a general assent to the terms of life which they, as the last receivers of tradition, had adopted at pain and cost.'

52. R. Banning & M. Quinn, *Djabugay Ngirrma*, p. 61.

53. W. E. H. Stanner, 'On Aboriginal Religion', *Oceania*, Vol. XXXIII, No. 4,

June 1963, p. 153: '(h) The main rites simulated events of the founding dramas, though in covert ways often difficult to perceive through the complex and crescive symbolisms. The rites followed a set liturgical formulary, and had the character of great celebrations, being made the repository of the highest products of imaginative, theatrical and material art. Each ritual occasion vivified in the minds of celebrants the first instituting of the culture, deepened the sense of continuity with men's beginnings, and reaffirmed the structures of existence. Inevitably they produced an archaist outlook, a reactionary temper, and a conservative impulse.'

54. W. E. H. Stanner, 'On Aboriginal Religion', *Oceania*, Vol. XXXIII, No. 4, June 1963, p. 154: '(k). To pass through the ritualized ordeals put a mark on the psychological, emotional, mental and social character of the initiates. It probably heightened their sense of ambient mystery and may have deepened their interior life. It certainly put them in fear of authority and taught them the value of social fellowship. The instructive artifices were extremely skilful. Throughout the ordeals fear was in some sense countered by security, isolation by comradeship, privation by sustenance, and pain by reward. A discovery of the dependency of life was eased by the revelation of things that could be celebrated joyfully. The dangers to life were relieved by a gift of the ritual means to assure its confident continuance. The end of the ordeal was the seal of manhood and the key to a man's privilege. All this was done in a context of high excitement, secrecy and beauty. Every man who came to full manhood did so, not only with no man's hand against him, but covered by the freely-given blood of a class of men who, though inherently opposed to him, depended on him as he did on them.'

55. E. Mjoberg, *Amongst Stone Age People in the Queensland Wilderness*, 1918, translated by S. M. Fryer for the John Oxley Library, 1986, p. 145.

56. C. Anderson, *The Political and Economic Basis of Kuku-Yalanji Social History*, p. 127.

57. W. E. Roth, *North Queensland Ethnography*, Bulletin 12, 1909, pp. 168–69.

58. *All Things Are Connected*, TBS Productions Inc., 1984 (U.S. TV Documentary).

CHAPTER 2   *FROM BAMA BULMBA TO FAR NORTH QUEENSLAND (1873–1912)*

1. Actually Cook as a mariner recorded that it was Sunday, 10 June, but a landsman would say it was Monday, 11 June 1770, see A. McInnes, 'Off Cairns—In the Week Commencing Trinity Sunday, 1770', *Historical Society of Cairns*, Bulletin No. 178, September 1974. Again, for the purposes of clarity, the 'corrected' landlubber way of dating has been used.

2. T. Bottoms, *The Bama—People of the Rainforest*, Gadja Enterprises, Cairns, 1992.

3. Jeffreys in *Kangaroo*, 1815; King in *Mermaid,* 1819; King in the *Bathurst,* 1821; Wickham in *Beagle*, 1839; Stokes in *Beagle*, 1841; Blackwood in *Fly*, 1843; Capt. M. McKenzie with Ludwig Leichhardt in the *Heroine*, February 1846; and Stanley in *Rattlesnake*, 1848.

4. J. W. Collinson, *Early Days of Cairns,* W. R. Smith & Paterson Pty Ltd, Brisbane, 1939, p. 2.

5. The course of the Barron River has 'migrated across the plain, on some occasions switching courses suddenly during major floods . . . An example of such a change in the river was witnessed during a cyclone in 1939. Before then the mouth was near Ellie Point, but during the floods the coastal sand spit south of Machan's Beach was cut through, and a new mouth formed further north.' W. F. Wilmott & P. J. Stephenson, *Rocks and Landscapes of the Cairns District*, Qld Dept of Mines, Brisbane, 1989, p. 20.

6. R. A. Johnstone, *Spinifex and Wattle—Reminiscences of Pioneering in North Queensland,* p. 5.

7. The term 'Gadja' referred to the spirit of a dead person, usually male, but has become a general term referring to Europeans.

8. Ibid., 23 May 1903, p. 8.

9. By Cook in 1770. The North East Coast Expedition arrived the day before the S. S. *Leichardt*; see 'Narrative and Reports of the Queensland North-East Coast Expedition 1873', *Queensland Votes and Proceedings,* S.1.V.2. 1874.

10. Official proclamation of the Hodgkinson Field was reported on 21 March 1876, D. Jones, *Trinity Phoenix,* Cairns, 1976, p. 48.

11. Some 70 miles (about 120 km) instead of 150 miles (about 260 km) to Cooktown.

12. 'Bird-Barrier Mountain'.

13. J. W. Collinson to T. Crowe, 24 March 1952, Collinson Papers, OM 73–62, No. 7, John Oxley Library.

14. Personal communication, Mrs Flo Williams, 30 September 1997.

15. Alan Broughton, 'The Douglas Track'—Excursion Notes, *Historical Society of Cairns,* 19 October 1980.

16. *Queensland State Archives*, TRE/A16 1876/1647.

17. *Queenslander,* 11 November 1876.

18. Ibid.

19. Sub-Inspector Douglas' 'good' character can be seriously challenged when taking into account a report by P. Cooper and V. Powers on 28 December 1880 to A. H. Palmer, Colonial Secretary, [*Queensland State Archives* COL/A 306 81/296], and the beatings he exacted on members of his Native Mounted Police troopers, as well as his predilection for Aboriginal women. An enquiry in 1885 by the MLA John Hamilton dismissed the NMP troopers' allegations, '[h]owever, the inquiry canvassed a number of other matters of some seriousness, involving dispersal of innocent Aboriginal camps, sexual abuse of Aboriginal women, ill-treatment of native troopers and procurement of alcohol and opium to win back their loyalty', N. Kirkman, 'The Palmer Gold Field 1873–1883', Honours Thesis, James Cook University, Townsville, 1984, pp. 302–5.

20. J. W. Collinson, 'Genesis of Cairns', *Historical Society of Cairns*, D1932, p. 2.

21. 'The New Road and Port', *Port Denison Times*, 14 October 1876.

22. *Cooktown Herald,* 7 October 1876.

23. 'Trinity Bay, Cairns, Nov. 9.', *Port Denison Times*, 25 November 1876; The main European form of transport was the horse, so it is not surprising that Bama targeted them. '4 horses belonging to a packer were speared by the

blacks at the Six Mile Creek, which is situated six miles below the second crossing of the Barron River. One horse died and the second had to be left on the spot.' *Cairns Advertiser,* 1 September 1877.

24. N. Kirkman, 'The Palmer Gold Field 1873–1883', p. 322.

25. *Port Denison Times*, 25 August 1877.

26. J. G. Winfield, 'The Hodgkinson Goldfields', *Historical Society of Cairns*, Bulletin 128, March 1970.

27. See *Queensland State Archives*, POL 12M/G1. The Native Mounted Police Force had operated in Victoria (1842) and in NSW (1848), and in the Moreton Bay district since 1853 (although it was another six years before this area became a part of the newly created colony of Queensland, in 1859). See R. Kidd, 'Regulating Bodies: administrations and Aborigines in Queensland 1840–1988', PhD Thesis, Griffith University, Brisbane, 1994, pp. 36–42; 'This force also became the legitimate instrument of government policy in Queensland. A European officer, sometimes a subordinate European officer, and a body of Aboriginal troopers ranging in numbers from four to ten. The Native Police had three duties: to break up—"disperse"—large assemblages of blacks, and at the same time to intimidate them by constant patrolling; to apprehend Aboriginal "criminals"; and to act as a punitive force for the local settlers. The *Maryborough Chronicle* [14 March 1861] explained . . . [that by] "[t]aking advantage of known hostility between the various tribes of Aborigines, and training their savageness rather than endeavouring to overcome it, able-bodied blacks belonging to one district are transferred to another 200 or 300 miles away, taught the use of firearms, fully equipped, and then, under the guidance of European officers . . . they are sent out with full licence to shoot and to destroy as many blacks as they can find".' Breslin, *Exterminate With Pride*, p. 54; Officers 'were forbidden to report in detail', *The Way We Civilise*, Brisbane, 1880, p. 3; see also W. Rosser, *Up Rode the Troopers: The Black Police in Queensland*, UQP, St Lucia, 1990, and H. Reynolds, *The Other Side of the Frontier*, Penguin, Ringwood, 1982.

28. See *Queensland State Archives*, COL/A139 (M1631)—complaints cited from selectors on the Barron River. One Mr Affleck (26 October 1888) wrote 'Blacks sperin [sic] Cattle down the River Saw 3 just dead 5 spered [sic]', while another selector wrote that '[t]he blacks have been spearing cattle on Bushy Creek about 3 miles from here during the last few Moonlight nights, can you send a detachment of the boys to patrole [sic] this part . . .'

29. Isley to Acting Commissioner of Police, 1 February 1881, *Queensland State Archives*, POL 12 M/G2.

30. H. Reynolds, *The Other Side of the Frontier*, Penguin, Ringwood, 1982, p. 78.

31. W. E. Parry-Okedon, 'Report on the North Queensland Aborigines and the Native Police', *Queensland Votes and Proceedings*, 1897, p. 38.

32. G. Pike, *Conquest of the Ranges*, Pinevale Publications, Mareeba, 1984, p. 49.

33. J. W. Collinson, 'Early Days of Cairns: The Aboriginals', *Cummins & Campbell's Monthly Magazine,* January, 1939, p. 9.

34. N. Loos, *Invasion and Resistance*, ANUP, Canberra, 1982, p. 228.

35. George Hobson was killed 'on his property, just opposite Myola Railway Station', on 20 July 1890. *Historical Society of Cairns*, Bulletin 158; one Bama, by the name of Darkie, was convicted of Hobson's murder and ended up on

Fraser Island, where '[i]n company with a countryman he embarked in a canoe and succeeded in reaching the main land, after which they walked to Ingham, and eventually reached Cairns by boat . . .' *Brisbane Telegraph*, 21 April 1902 from *Cairns Morning Post*, 11 April 1902; Darkie was re-arrested by Constable Barson of Kuranda, and was sent south, eventually ending up in Darundur, near Caboolture.

36. See J. Cairns & W. T. Johnston, *Port Douglas: A History-Sketch Record*, Atherton, 1986, 'The Old Bump Road', p. 6, for details.

37. See Appendix A, in T. Bottoms, 'Djarrugan—The Last of the Nesting'; also C. R. McCracken, 'Some Walking Tracks . . .', *Queensland Archaeological Research*, Vol. 6, 1989, p. 110.

38. *Cooktown Herald*, 29 July 1877.

39. J. W. Collinson, 'Rise and Decline of Port Douglas', *Journal of the Royal Historical Society of Queensland*, Vol. 4, No. 4, December 1951, pp. 563–64.

40. J. W. Collinson, *Early Days of Cairns*, W. R. Smith & Paterson Pty Ltd, Brisbane, 1939, p. 106.

41. C. Lack, 'The Town That Was Drowned', *Journal of the Royal Historical Society of Queensland*, Vol. 9, No. 2, 1970–71, p. 234; *Port Denison Times*, 12 April 1879.

42. Bill Smith shot and killed Robert Craig on Boxing Day, 1877, then turned the gun on himself. *Cooktown Herald*, 29 December 1877.

43. D. M. Connolly, *Chronicles of Mowbray and Port Douglas*, Cairns, 1984, p. 44.

44. Ibid.

45. Ibid.

46. P. Savage, 'The Second Diary: Herberton to the Coast, 1882', *Christie Palmerston Explorer*, Records of North Queensland History No. 2, James Cook University, Townsville, 1989, pp. 89–121.

47. Ibid., p. 109; A present-day bush walker and expert on the Barron Gorge, Alan Broughton, agrees with his judgment.

48. Ibid., p. 110.

49. R. F. Ellis, *Rails to the Tableland*, Australian Railway Historical Society, Brisbane, 1985, pp. 11–12.

50. *Cairns Post*, 15 January 1885.

51. *Yilbong* or *Millbong*'s association with Pine River suggests that he was a member of the Undanbi nation (of the coastal area immediately to the north of Brisbane).

52. Constance Campbell Petrie, *Tom Petrie's Reminiscences of Early Queensland*, Brisbane, 1904, Lloyd O'Niel, Hawthorn, 1975, p. 169.

53. *Cairns Post*, 10 May 1886.

54. *Cairns Post*, 14 October 1886.

55. *Cairns Post*, 28 October 1886. Whelan was apparently a Senior Constable, not a Sergeant. Staff List, Mulgrave River Native Mounted Police Camp, 1885–89, Queensland Police Museum.

56. Personal communication from Kelvin A. Hill to author in letter dated 17 July 1990.

57. *Cairns Post*, 21 May 1887.

58. A. D. Broughton & S. E. Stephens, *Establishment of Trinity Bay*, Historical Society of Cairns, Cairns, 1984, p. 27.

59. *Cairns Post*, 8 June 1887.

60. R. F. Ellis, *Rails to the Tableland*, p. 13.

61. *Cairns Post*, 8 June 1887.

62. *Cairns Post*, 19 November 1887. Senior Constable Whelan was in the Native Mounted Police.

63. *Cairns Post*, 18 February 1888.

64. See Chapter 2 'Bama Bulurru', and Chapter 3 'The Bulmba of the Bama', in T. Bottoms, 'Djarrugan—The Last of the Nesting'.

65. *Cairns Post*, 8 February 1888.

66. *Cairns Post*, 21 March 1888.

67. R. F. Ellis, *Rails to the Tableland*, p. 16.

68. *Queenslander*, 8 December 1877, p. 16.

69. Police Commissioner's Report of 1878, *Queensland Votes and Proceedings*, 1879, p. 752.

70. Douglas to Isley, 1 March 1878; Douglas to Isley, 26 November 1878; *Queensland State Archives*, POL 12 M/G1.

71. *Cairns Post*, 7 August 1884. Sub-Inspector Carr was stationed at the Upper Barron River Native Mounted Police camp of Baan Bêro, six kilometres north, northwest of the present Biboohra, from 1879 until April 1886. The site of Baan Bêro appears to have been chosen by Inspector Isley in 1877 (Isley to Commissioner of Police, 6 October, 1884, *Queensland State Archives* Police Department, Commissioner's Office, Police Stations, A 41603 403S 84/578), and was operational in January 1878 with Sub-Inspector Alex Douglas in-charge (*Queensland State Archives*, POL 12/G1). In 1887 Bishop Gilbert White described the officer's house as standing 'on top of a hill, about 100 feet high [about 30 m], which has been cleared of timber. Below are the quarters of the troopers and the stables. Close by is a large paddock with two large lagoons covered with waterfowl. The view is superb. You see over a great plain covered with trees to the blue mountains, which rise fifteen or twenty miles away on every side.' Bishop G. White in J. O. Feetham & W. V. Rymer (eds), *North Queensland Jubilee Book 1878–1928*, The Diocese of North Queensland, Townsville, 1929, p. 112. Sub-Inspector Garraway was Officer in charge in 1888, and the Camp Sergeant was Constable Arundel, *North Queensland Register*, 25 March 1933.

72. '[I]t was a strategic position as regards the cattlemen, the teamsters, the miners and the settlers. It was within easy reach of Cairns, Tinaroo, Herberton, Thornborough and Port Douglas. It was [also] near the junction of three telegraph lines.' J. W. Collinson to Tom Crowe (Mareeba), 24 March 1952. John Oxley Library, Collinson Papers, OM 73–62, No. 7.

73. Atherton to Colonial Secretary, 10 December 1878, *Queensland State Archives*, A/268, 78/4602. After Atherton's first tin samples were tested in Cairns, a small rush set in. See D. Jones, *Trinity Phoenix*, p. 137. It is worth noting that Sub-Inspector Douglas, in a report dated 15 November 1878, to the Commissioner of Police, stated that 'he had a long conversation with Mr. Atherton the largest squatter up here and a neighbour of mine. He and I are going to gather as many gins etc. as we possibly can and keep them for a time, letting them work with the troopers and their gins about the place, gradually letting a few go away from time to time so as to try and induce

the blacks to come in also. Our idea is keep these gins say for a week up at Mr. Atherton's station and for the same period or more here [Baan Bêro].' *Queensland State Archives*, COL A/306 81/296. Had they implemented this, it would have caused a great deal of conflict with the Bama warriors, and may account for the problems that Atherton later experienced.

74. Turning off the Kennedy Highway onto Speewah Road, just over the bridge on the left-hand side. See *Queenslander*, 26 October 1878; 'The road to the foot of the Range via Smithfield (being also the main road to Thornborough & Tinaroo) needs immediate attention . . . men to work on the road from Grove's selection to Tinaroo', A. Dennis (Secretary, Cairns Road Board) to Under Secretary of Public Works, 12 July 1879, ff. *Queensland State Archives*, Register of Letters Received, 1879–80, WOR/A 206, 81/3582; *Queensland State Archives*, WOR/N5 1880–91, single sheet (no number) memo of expenditure; *Queensland Votes and Proceedings*, 1880, Vol. 2, p. 994, both confirm expenditure; see also Survey 1 November 1883 by Surveyor Gwynne, Cat. No. C153.65 & C153.53; Ryan, Hunt, Burtle & Tolson to Chairman & members of the Cairns Divisional Board, regarding a £50 subsidy for 'two men and a camp keeper . . . to explore the coast range', 26 October 1880; note confirming previous day's £50 'bonus', 27 October 1880, *Cairns Divisional Board Letterbook*.

75. Letter dated 5 September 1881, *Queensland State Archives*, POL 12M/G2.

76. W. T. Johnstone, 'A Town with so much to Recall', *Sunday Mail Color*, 14 November 1976; 'Tramp', 'The Path of the Pioneers', *Cummins & Campbell's Monthly Magazine*, May 1936, pp. 13–15; J. Black, *North Queensland Pioneers*, CWA, Charters Towers, 1931, p. 75.

77. T. Bottoms, 'Djarrugan—The Last of the Nesting', p. 45A.

78. 'Tramp', *Cummins & Campbell's Monthly Magazine*, May 1936, pp. 13–15.

79. Ibid., p. 45.

80. D. M. Connolly, *Chronicles of Mowbray and Port Douglas*, June, 1984, p. 45.

81. See the *Cook District, 2 Mile Map Sheet No. 1, Port Douglas & Neighbourhood*, The Surveyor General's Office, Brisbane, September 1894.

82. 'There was a massacre up there too . . . It wasn't the settlers who shot the Bama, it was the Police . . .' Mrs Enid Boyle, 3 October 1997.

83. A series of articles in *Cairns Argus* and *Cairns Post* in 1890 and 1891 refer obliquely to a massacre, particularly their discussion of one Professor Rentoul and Rev. John Gribble's visit to Kuranda. Referring to Prof. Rentoul 'he considers the Hobson [see endnote 35] tragedy was followed by tragedies of perhaps even a more terrible character, and that it is not improbable that lives were taken perhaps of innocent persons in avenging poor Hobson's death . . . for the stories that reached Professor Rentoul are open secrets in Cairns'. *Cairns Argus*, 22 August 1890. Hobson died on 20 July 1890. This might therefore suggest that the Snake Gully/Speewah massacre occurred in late July 1890. Buttercup and her mother Minnie escaped by following *djumburru* (walking pads) down to Freshwater Creek. They sought and found refuge with the Gadja Banning family.

84. Interview in *Walsh and Tinaroo Miner*, 24 December 1907, cited in G. C. Bolton, *A Thousand Miles Away*, ANUP, Canberra, 1972, p. 94. If Atherton's statement is true, then he lost 1826 bullocks over five years (allowing for one

leap year). He had stocked his selection with 1600 head of cattle (J. Black, *North Queensland Pioneers*, CWA, Charters Towers, 1931, p. 4). While his losses may have been pronounced, one might suggest, say hypothetically one bullock a week for five years, this would be equivalent of 209 beasts, which is not the dramatic figure which Atherton projects.

85. *Cairns Post*, 7 August 1884.

86. Buttercup and *Binda Nyiwul* (Tambo Banning) brought their family up on Andrew Banning's selection. Andrew Banning was an American who took possession of his selection in the Freshwater Valley after 1886. *Cairns Post* 6 January 1892 reported that ninety-eight acres had been cleared and that he lived in an impressive house. Descendants of the Bama Bannings still live at Redlynch.

87. Personal communication, Glen Williams, Senior Djabugay Ranger.

88. Personal communication, Elder, Selwyn Hunter, 19 September 1995, and others.

89. Personal communication, Elder, Florence Williams, 18 September 1998.

90. 'Aborigines of Queensland', *Queensland Votes and Proceedings*, 1874, p. 440.

91. S. Humston, *Kuranda—The Village in the Rainforest 1888–1988*, Brisbane, 1988, p. 22.

92. Cook District 2 Mile Sketch Map Sheet No. 5—Cairns, Herberton, Mulgrave River, 1886 (NG1).

93. D. Jones, *Trinity Phoenix*, Cairns, p. 288.

94. R. L. Sharp, 'Tribes and Totemism in North-East Australia', *Oceania*, Vol. 9, 1938/9, p. 446.

95. *Cairns Argus*, 22 August 1890.

96. Ibid.

97. By 12 April 1891, Kuranda had been reached, and Myola by 13 May 1891. See R. F. Ellis, *Rails to the Tableland*, pp. 21–22.

98. At least 126 selections had been made and recorded on the 1891 *Queensland Census Districts*, No. 9 Map of Cairns.

99. *Cairns Post*, 25 February, 11 April 1891.

100. In the court case *Regina v. Darkie*, investigating the murder of G. Hobson, it was acknowledged that 'about a mile further up the [Barron] river from Hobson's a large camp of blacks, 50 or 60 . . .', Cairns Circuit Court, 2 April 1891, *Queensland State Archives*, COL/143 M 1634 (z1610), p. 3.

101. J. B. Gribble, *Diary of J. B. Gribble*, 23/24 August 1891, p. 13, Mitchell Library N–3.

102. Lady Knox travelled under the alias of Ellis Rowan; E. Rowan, *The Flower Hunter*, Angus & Robertson, North Ryde, 1898, pp. 42, 45–46.

103. *Cairns Post*, 8 August 1891.

104. Ibid., 7024, with 5344 males and 1680 females.

105. It is difficult to give exact figures of Bama population numbers, but Sub-Inspector A. D. Douglas in 1878 stated to the Commissioner of Police that '[a]t the lowest computation there must be at least 4,000 and out of this number 3,000 may be put down as actually belonging to the coast', Alexander D. Douglas, letter from Baan Bêro, 15 November 1878, *Queensland State Archives*, COL/A306, 81/296. It seems likely that Douglas is referring to the districts around Cairns, to the north and west, which appear to be his area of jurisdiction. Assuming that his estimate is for only part of the area delineated

by the approximate boundaries of the Djabugay/Yidiny-speaking Bama (see Map 2) of the Cairns rainforest region, then a possible conservative estimate might suggest that 4000 to 5000 people is a fair deduction.

106. S. Humston, *Kuranda—The Village in the Rainforest 1888–1988*, p. 33.
107. Ibid.; Personal communication with Mrs Florence Williams, 4 August 1985.
108. S. Humston, *Kuranda—The Village in the Rainforest 1888–1988*, p. 35.
109. A. Meston, 'Report on the Aboriginals of Queensland', *Queensland Votes and Proceedings*, 1896, p. 732.
110. N. Loos, *Invasion and Resistance*, p. 109–11.
111. A. Meston, *Queensland Votes and Proceedings*, 1896, p. 733.
112. G. Genever, 'Black and Blue: Aboriginal–Police Relations in Early Far North Queensland', *Historical Society of Cairns*, Bulletin 402, May 1994.

CHAPTER 3 *MISSION DAYS (1913–1962)*

1. *Queensland Parliamentary Papers*, 1913, p. 1073; This was probably Street Creek/Barron Falls Camp, located near the junction of Street Creek and the Barron River, just above *Din Din* (Barron Falls) on the northern bank of the river (see Map 6).
2. P. B. Rudge, 'Article', *Australasian Record*, 22 September 1913, p. 8. The Seventh Day Adventist Union applied to the Queensland Minister for Home Affairs on 17 March 1913, and five months later, in September, the task began; see also *Cairns Post*, 15 May 1914. One Sub-Inspector W. Cooper was sent in May 1898 at the behest of the Premier, T. J. Byrnes, to find out 'the feelings of the Cairns District with regard to amending the Aboriginal Act . . .' and apparently interviewed 'fully 500 blacks at different camps between Cairns and the Tate [River]' assuring them 'that the Government wished to be their friend and that they would not be removed from their own country but that able bodied ones must get work where possible'. He concludes that the 'idea of shifting Blacks on to any given Reserve would not I respectfully suggest, be a success' and goes on to say that local whites were against a proposed reserve at Kamerunga. See 'Letter from Sub Insp. W. Cooper in Cairns, 3 June, 1898', *Queensland State Archives*, COL/A139.
3. M. Quinn, *Galing Munu-Munu-La*, Mona Mona Aboriginal Corporation, Cairns, 1994, p. 1.
4. P. B. Rudge, 'Monamona and the Natives', *Australasian Record*, 26 January 1914, pp. 2–3.
5. P. B. Rudge, 'Monamona Mission', *Australasian Record*, 9 March 1914, p. 5.
6. Branford to Chief Protector Bleakley, 13 September 1914, *Queensland State Archives*, A/58784 1913–1933.
7. Ibid., Chief Protector to Superintendent, Monamona Mission, 24 September, 1914.
8. J. W. Bleakley, 'Annual Report of the Chief Protector of Aboriginals for the Year 1915', *Queensland Parliamentary Papers*, 1916.
9. K. McDonald Grant, Home Secretary of the State of Queensland, 'Order For Removal of Aboriginals', 19 April 1915, *Home Secretary's Office*, 03671, 13 April 1915.

10. *Djabugay Oral History Program*, Interview with Mr Warren Brim, Bare Hill, 25 April 1994.

11. A. J. Hillier, 'The Native Police under Scrutiny', *Journal of the Royal Historical Society of Queensland*, Vol. XV, No. 6, February, 1994, p. 288.

12. Oral History Interview with Mr Selwyn Hunter, 3 August 1995.

13. A report to the Chief Protector referring to the Kuranda Bama stated that '[t]his tribe so far has resisted the persuasion of the Missionaries at Monamona to join the Mission and I feel confident the white residents are chiefly responsible for this. Many of them have found the men very profitable servants at the absurd wage of 3/- or 5/- a week and at the time of my visit were complaining of the hardship caused by the direction of the local protector that half wages were to be banked.' Attached to letter from Branford to Chief Protector, 13 September 1914, *Queensland State Archives*, A/58784 1913–1933.

14. Letter dated 5 March 1916, and telegram 6 March 1916, from Hunter to Theodore, Member of the Legislative Assembly, *Queensland State Archives*, A/69429—General Correspondence of the Chief Protector of Aboriginals, *Seventh Day Adventists Archives*, Removal of Kuranda Natives to Mona Mona.

15. Telegram to McCormack, Member of the Legislative Assembly, 10 March 1916, *Queensland State Archives*, A/69429.

16. William Gall, Under Secretary of the Home Secretary's Office, Brisbane, to the Hon. W. McCormack, Member of the Legislative Assembly, 14 March 1916, *Queensland State Archives*, A/69429, *Seventh Day Adventist Archives*, Removal of Kuranda Natives to Mona Mona.

17. '[I]t would be better if all these natives were rounded up and sent out to Monamona Reserve, where I have no doubt they would soon become contented and settle down. This would certainly be better for them than hanging round the town or working at starvation wages. If such removal should be carried out, it would be necessary to provide a sufficiently large escort to carry out the removal all together and also conveyances for their luggage and effects.' Report with letter 13 September 1914, *Queensland State Archives*, A/58784.

18. *Djabugay Oral History Program*, interview at Bare Hill with Mr. W. Brim, 25 April 1995.

19. S. Humston, *Kuranda—The Village in the Rainforest 1888–1998*, p. 49.

20. Ibid.

21. D. Bowman, Home Secretary of the State of Queensland, 'Order For the Removal of Aboriginals', 10 February 1916. *Seventh Day Adventist Archives*, Removal of Kuranda Natives to Mona Mona.

22. M. Quinn, *Galing Munu-Munu-La*, p. 4.

23. S. Collins, 'Mona Mona: A Culture in Transition', Grad. Dip. Material Culture, James Cook University, Townsville, 1981.

24. Ibid.; J. Cochran, 'One House in Malanda: Life Histories of Three Aboriginal Women in Queensland', 14 May 1993, *Historical Society of Cairns*, 305 COC; *Seventh Day Adventist Archives*, Removal of Kuranda Natives to Mona Mona.

25. J. W. Bleakley, *Queensland Parliamentary Papers,* 1916 (for 1915).

26. 'Mona Mona Mission', *Queensland Parliamentary Papers*, 1920 (for 1919).

27. *Queensland State Archives*, Box 730 R254 6J/13.

28. Personal communication, Mrs Florence Williams, 16 September 1997.

29. S. Collins, 'Mona Mona: A Culture in Transition', 1981.

30. Personal communication, Mrs Enid Boyle, 16 September 1997.

31. Ibid.

32. Dr N. B. Tindale, Diary Notes Sunday, 28 August 1938, Harvard Adelaide Universities Anthropological Expedition, South Australian Museum.

33. Personal communication, Mrs Enid Boyle, 16 September 1997.

34. *Cairns Post*, 28 March 1913; this included parts of a timber reserve, S. Collins, 'Mona Mona: A Culture in Transition', 1981.

35. D. Connolly, *Chronicles of Mowbray and Port Douglas*, Cairns, June 1984, p. 45.

36. Memorandum from O'Leary, Deputy Chief Protector of Aboriginals to Superintendent, Mona Mona Mission, 26 April 1934, *Seventh Day Adventist Archives*.

37. E. M. Hanlon, Home Secretary, Order for Removals of Aboriginals, 21 May 1934, No. 31, *Seventh Day Adventist Archives*.

38. '[T]he intention of turning around'—WARRN.GI-Y, see M. Quinn, *Djabugay—A Djabugay-English Dictionary*, Qld Dept of Education, Cairns, 1992, p. 68.

39. *Warringinya* (Fanny) died at Monamona Mission in July 1934. Mission Records—Original Aboriginal roll Revised 30 June 1934, p. 32, *Seventh Day Adventist Archives*.

40. *Queensland Parliamentary Papers*, 1920 (for 1919) £500 worth of food has been raised (home consumption); 1922 (for 1921) Plantation—70 tons sweet potatoes (home consumption), 6 acres cassava, 8 acres more 'coming on well'; 1923 (for 1922) 'satisfactory crop returns'; 1925 (for 1924) 80 tons sweet potatoes, 1000 banana suckers planted, amongst other things; 1929 (for 1928) Crops valued at £500. 'This was apart from the private kitchen gardens of the inmates'; 1930 (for 1929) Produce valued at £550; 1931 (for 1930) Produce valued at £600; 1934 (for 1933) 'natives are easily 75 percent self-supporting'; 1936 (for 1935) 'ample food crops were produced from the farms'.

41. *Queensland Parliamentary Papers*, 1932 (for 1931).

42. Ibid.

43. *Queensland Parliamentary Papers*, 1922 (for 1921)—'The earnings of two fine bullock teams hauling timber have contributed largely to the support of the station'; 1923 (for 1922) 'Sawmill and bullock teams contributed an important part of mission revenue'; 1925 (for 1924) 'Timber-getting and sawmilling principal revenue of £2,000'; 1926 (for 1925) timber-getting and sawmilling 'the products of which find a ready sale and make this settlement practically self-supporting'; 1931 (for 1930) timber hauling main support—'Depression seriously affected source of revenue'; 1932 (for 1931) timber hauling valued at £700; 1934 (for 1933)—timber logging operations constitute main source of revenue.

44. *Cairns Post*, 21 March 1934.

45. J. Campbell, District Secretary of the Australian Workers' Union to the Chief Protector of Aboriginals, 27 September 1927, *Queensland State Archives*, A/58861, Monamona 1927–1934.

46. *Queensland State Archives*, A/34/2473, Chief Protector to Under Secretary, Home Dept, 17 May 1934.

47. *Queensland Parliamentary Papers*, 1939 (for 1938).

48. U. H. McConnel, 'Cape York Peninsula: (3) Development and Control', *Walkabout*, August 1936, p. 36.

49. Personal communication, Mr S. Fagan, 31 July 1995.

50. 'When Palm Island was being considered as a new Aboriginal reserve during the years of World War I, Chief Protector J. Bleakley wrote to the Under Home Secretary: "A reserve is needed for use as a penitentiary for troublesome cases and to which aboriginals from the Northern districts can be removed . . . A most suitable place in my opinion would be Great Palm Island, north of Townsville, which some time ago on my application was reserved for Aboriginals.' R. Evans, K. Saunders & K. Cronin, *Race Relations in Colonial Queensland*, UQP, St Lucia, 1993, p. 349.

51. Personal communication, M. & S. Fagan, 31 July 1995. E. H. Short recalled life on the southern Tableland, and wrote of the Bama, that '[t]hey were terrified of being sent to mission stations, and for some reason Palm Island was regarded as the ultimate hell. I have seen an Aboriginal who was threatened with Palm Island cringe, roll his eyes, turn several shades lighter with sheer terror and fairly shiver. I suspect that the Police used Mission Stations and Palm Island in particular to keep them in line.' *The Nation Builders*, Brisbane, 1988, pp. 61–62.

52. *Queensland State Archives*, Box 729, R254, 6J/5 Transfer Mission Site.

53. Memorandum from Deputy Supervisor of the Aboriginal Hospital, Fantome Island to Director of Native Affairs, 10 October 1940; Ibid.

54. S. Collins, 'Mona Mona: A Culture in Transition', pp. 17 & 56.

55. Personal communication, Mrs W. Brim, 1 August 1995; 'Borgas had lots of different size canes for different offences and people', Mr M. Brim, 10 September 1997.

56. Personal communication, Mrs J. Donohue, Mareeba, 8 August 1995.

57. Personal communication, Mrs W. Brim, Mantaka, 1 August 1995.

58. Ibid.

59. Ibid.

60. Personal communication, Mr S. Fagan, Cairns, 31 July 1995.

61. J. Cochran, 'One House in Malanda: Life Histories of Three Aboriginal Women in Queensland', *Historical Society of Cairns*, 14 May 1993, 305 COC, p. 26.

62. M. Quinn, *Galing Munu-Munu-La*, p. 4.

63. Oral History Program—Mrs Marita Hobbler to Rosetta Brim, Mona Mona, 15 July 1997.

64. Personal communication, Mrs W. Brim, 1 August 1995.

65. Mrs M. Hobbler recorded by W. Brim, in M. Breslin (Co-Ordinator), *Remembering: Interviews of Aboriginal Community Members by Smithfield High Aboriginal Students,* Queensland Education Department, Cairns, 1992, p. 17.

66. Personal communication, Mr Lyn Hobbler, 3 August 1995; Mrs W. Brim, Mantaka, 1 August 1995.

67. H. A. Borland, *Roadway of Many Memories 1876–1951*, Cairns District Jubilee Souvenir, Cairns, 1951, pp. 24–29.

68. Norman Tindale's Diary, Sunday August 28, 1938, South Australian Museum, Anthropology Department, Adelaide, p. 321.

69. Personal communication, Mr Steven Fagan, 27 February 1998.

70. R. Cilento, Director Gen. Health & Home Affairs, 'Visit of Inspection to Palm Island, Yarrabah and Mona Mona Aboriginal Settlements, Feb–Mar 1937, *Queensland State Archives*, 37/5698 A/58784.

71. Dr G. Croll's Report, 28 April 1939, *Queensland State Archives*, Box 729 6J/9.

72. P. Ludlow, *The Exiles of Peel Island—Leprosy*, Stones Corner, 1991, p. 29.

73. The Brisbane *Telegraph*, 7 April 1937; 'Last year 14 lepers including 8 whites, were admitted to Peel Island lazaret . . . Seventy lepers were inmates . . . 24 whites and 46 coloured people. In 1936–7 there were 74 inmates', *Courier Mail*, 12 October 1938. See also J. Maguire, 'The Fantome Island Leprosarium', in R. MacLeod & D. Denoon (Eds), *Health & Healing in Tropical Australia and Papua New Guinea*, James Cook University, Townsville, 1991, pp. 142–48.

74. 'By 1948, Dr Reyes was spending six weeks at Peel, alternating with six weeks at Fantome Island. Prior to this, Fantome Island had been under the medical care of the Medical Officer at Palm Island. The Queensland Government spent about £1,000 per year on each white patient at Peel Island, which is in sharp contrast to the roughly £100 per year spent on each aboriginal patient at Fantome Island. Failure to obtain approval to construct adequate quarters for his patients at Fantome led to Dr Reyes' resignation at the end of 1949.' P. Ludlow, *The Exiles of Peel Island—Leprosy*, 1991, p. 53.

75. R. Cilento to the Minister, Dept Health & Home Affairs, 30 November, 1939, *Queensland State Archives*, Box 729, 6J/5.

76. H. E. Piper, Sec. Australasian Union Conference (SDA) to Dir. Native Affairs, 3 February 1941, ibid.

77. Personal communication, F. Williams, Kowrowa, 4 August 1995.

78. M. Quinn, *Galing Munu-Munu-La*, p. 5.

79. R. Sheppard, *Djabugay Oral History Program*, taped interview recorded 26 June 1994.

80. Personal communication, Lyn Hobbler, Mantaka, 3 August 1995.

81. Personal communication, M. & S. Fagan, Cairns, 31 July 1995.

82. Ibid.

83. Mrs Emma Snyder, interviewed by J. Cochran, 'One House in Malanda', p. 31.

84. Personal communication, Lorna Mitchell, Mareeba, 8 August 1995.

85. *Queensland Parliamentary Papers*, 1943, p. 685.

86. Personal communication, G. Donohue, Mareeba, 8 August 1995.

87. Personal communication, W. Brim, Mantaka, 1 August 1995.

88. Personal communication, G. Donohue, Mareeba, 8 August 1995.

89. Personal communication, M. & S. Fagan, Cairns, 31 July 1995.

90. V. Bradley, *I didn't know that*, Boolarong Press, Moorooka, 1995, p. 374.

91. Between Scott and Severin Streets.

92. Lieut Fred Uyterwijk, in V. Bradley, *I didn't know that*, pp. 374–75.

93. Personal communication, V. Bradley, Cairns, 14 August 1995.

94. Cannon states 'that "voodoo death" may be real, and that it may be explained as due to shocking emotional stress—to obvious or repressed terror', p. 180. W. B. Cannon, '"Voodoo" Death', *American Anthropologist*, Vol. 44, April–June 1942, No. 2, pp. 169–81. See also W. E. Roth, 'Queensland Aboriginals', *Queenslander*, 28 February 1903; G. K. Alley, *Riverstone 1877–1977*, *Cairns Post*, p. 8, private publication held by the author.

95. Personal communication, S. Hunter, Kuranda, 3 August 1995.

96. Personal communication, Elder, Grandad Selwyn Hunter.

97. M. Quinn, *Galing Munu-Munu-La,* p. 11.

98. *Queensland Parliamentary Papers,* 1947/8, p. 1107.

99. *Queensland Parliamentary Papers,* 1948/9, p. 871.

100. *Queensland Parliamentary Papers,* 1949, p. 898.

101. Personal communication, S. Fagan, Cairns, 31 July 1995. By March 1952 the Mission was operating 'three vehicles: an Austin Lorry [paid for by DNA—£846/5/- in 1951], a 1936 D50 International and a 1949 V8 car. The Austin Lorry transports our personell [sic] to & from Cairns and Mareeba hospital, our supplies from Cairns and occassionally [sic] loads of goods from the mission. The D50 International is used only on very rare occasions, such as a 5–8 ton load. We have had it on the road only two or three times this year. The car is for use of the superintendent and is used in connection with his work also rush trips to hospital with an urgent patient.' *Queensland State Archives,* Box 730, R254 6J/16, W. E. Zanotti to Dep. Dir. Native Affairs, 19 March 1952.

102. Personal communication, Mrs Winnie Brim, at Ngoonbi Farm, 16 September 1997.

103. D. Blanch, 'Life Sketch of Pastor J. A. B. Blanch', written for his funeral in September 1982, p. 1.

104. *Queensland Parliamentary Papers,* 1951/52.

105. *Queensland Parliamentary Papers,* 1959/60.

106. The Superintendents were: W. Zanotti, G. J. Dawson, Pastor W. H. Turner, M. O. Bryde, and W. G. Petersen. *Queensland State Archives,* Box 730, R254 6J/13.

107. Report 227, January 1953, *Queensland State Archives,* Box 730 6J/19; see also J. Gillespie, 'The Hookworm Campaign', in J. MacLeod & D. Denoon (Eds), *Health and Healing in Tropical Australia and Papua New Guinea,* James Cook University, Townsville, 1991, pp. 64–87.

108. Hookworm Control, Cairns, to Sec. Dir. Gen. Health, 25 October 1962, *Queensland State Archives,* Box 730 6J/19.

109. Personal communication, M. Fagan, Cairns, 31 July 1995. The child endowment monies could well have been incorporated into the beleagured revenues of the Mission.

110. Dep. Dir. Native Affairs to Minister for Health & Home Affairs, 16 December 1941; Memorandum to Under Sec. 23 December 1941; & Dir. O'Leary of Native Affairs to Acting Under Sec., Dept Health & Home Affairs, 21 January 1942; *Queensland State Archives,* Box 729, 6J/9.

111. Dir. Native Affairs to Ferris, 1 March 1957, 12 March 1957, (to Mr Murphy, Accountant), 12 March 1957; 10 March 1957, *Queensland State Archives,* Box 729 6J/3.

112. Memo for file, O'Leary 5 March 1957, *Queensland State Archives,* Box 729 6J/3.

113. Letter from the President of the North Queensland Conference [SDA] to O'Leary, Director of Native Affairs, 9 July 1958. Pastor Ferris was fatally injured on 7 July 1958 'within four miles of Townsville . . . opposite the Ross River Meatworks', *Queensland State Archives,* Box 730 6J/13.

114. Ibid.

115. *Queensland State Archives*, Box 729 R254, 6J/13, Medical Superintendent to Dir. Gen. of Health & Medical Services, 15 October 1958.

116. F. Grogan, *Djabugay Oral History Program*, 6 July 1994.

117. T. G. Genever, 'Black and Blue: Aboriginal–Police Relations in Far North Queensland During the Currency of The Aboriginals Protection and the Restriction of the Sale of Opium Act, 1897–1939', BA(Hons) Thesis, James Cook University, Townsville, 1992, p. 92.

118. Personal communication, Mr Finlay Grogan, 5 August 1997.

119. Ibid.

120. Confidential interview with the 'lad' at the age of sixty-eight, 10 September 1997.

121. Ibid. There can be no doubt that the 'lad' is correct. European interpretations of inter-ethnic romance confirm this. For example, the Portuguese in Brazil viewed this as 'always a one-way affair: white male and Indian female, but never the other way around, white female with Indian male', A. Ramos, 'From Eden to limbo: the construction of indigenism in Brazil', in G. Clement Bond, & A. Gilliam, *Social Construction of the Past—Representation as Power*, Routledge, London, 1994, p. 78. R. W. Stedman, *Shadows of the Indians*, University of Oklahoma Press, Norman, 1987, gives examples of this in North America.

122. T. G. Genever, 'Black and Blue'.

123. Personal communication, Mrs W. Brim, Mantaka, 1 August 1995.

124. The damming of Flaggy Creek was first suggested in a 1945 Committee Report on 'Water Supply and Hydro-electric Power for the Cairns–Tully Regions'. A part of its conclusion stated that '[a] large storage capacity can be obtained without submerging land of high value, although it will be necessary to remove the buildings of the Monamona aboriginal mission to another site in the valley'. Four years later Mission people had expressed anxiety to the Department of Native Affairs 'regarding the possibility of part of the Reserve being inundated by water conservation schemes'. This concern was dispelled by the State Electricity Commission when they wrote that '[v]ery definitely there are no plans for immediate or early development'. *Queensland State Archives*, Box 730 R254 6J/16, Acting Sec. State Electricity Commission to President SDA, 22 December 1949; nine years later the Church (1 December 1958) and State Authorities (15 October 1958) were aware that Mona Mona was going to close due to part of the reserve (1040 acres) being submerged. *Queensland State Archives*, Box 729 R254 6J/8.

125. Official correspondence reflects this. For example, in July 1955 '[o]ur budget expenditure for all purposes total £20,500, so that with the £11,500 [cash from the Church] . . . together with the Government subsidy of £4,000 and child endowment £2,000, equalling £17,500, we still have a cash deficit of £3,000'. *Queensland State Archives*, Box 730 R254 6J/16.

126. In the final days, government subsidies, apart from other material assistance given, involved £15,000 a year from 1959 to 1962, plus half that for the last six months—a total of £52,000 over the last three years of the Mission's operations. Ibid., 6J/13.

127. *Queensland Parliamentary Papers*, 1961/62, p. 1356; *Queensland Parliamentary*

Papers, 1960/61, p. 1193: 'Employment: There is an increasing willingness on the part of natives to take work outside the Mission.'

128. Personal communication, Mrs M. Fagan, Cairns, 31 July 1995.

129. Personal communication, Mrs Jessie Donohue, Mareeba, 8 August 1995.

130. R. Sheppard, *Djabugay Oral History Program*.

131. Personal communication, Mrs W. Brim, Mantaka, 1 August 1995.

132. 'Report on Mona Mona Mission', L. McDonald, Community Relations Officer, 31 July 1984, *Queensland State Archives*, Box 729 6J/8.

133. S. Collins, 'Mona Mona', 1981.

134. Insp. Hookworm Control, Cairns, to Dir. Native Affairs, 25 October 1962, *Queensland State Archives*, Box 730 R254 6J/19.

135. Personal communication, Rhonda Brim, Mantaka, 17 August 1995. Confirmed by Dir. Native Affairs to Superintendent, 28 December 1962, *Queensland State Archives*, Box 729 6J/8.

136. J. Boswell, 'The Life of Samuel Johnson LL.D 1791', Part One, in *Library of the Future* (Third Edition), World Library, Inc., Irvine, CA, 1993.

CHAPTER 4 *THIS SIDE OF THE RAILWAY TRACKS (1963–1997)*

1. Report on Mona Mona Mission, *Queensland State Archives*, Box 729 6J/8. During the mission period, the name was 'Monamona' but, since the demise of the mission, the Djabugay refer to the site as 'Mona Mona'.

2. Memo, around 2 June 1961, *Queensland State Archives*, Box 729 6J/8.

3. Dan Coleman, Bama representative cited by the Trans-Tasman Union Conference of SDA 9 June 1961 to Dir. Native Affairs, ibid.

4. Trans-Tasman Union Conference of the SDA, 9 June 1961 to Dir. Native Affairs, ibid.

5. Dir. Native Affairs to Sec. Co-ord. Gen. Public Works, 15 October 1960, ibid.

6. Trans-Tasman letter 9 June 1961, op. cit.

7. Memo 7 June 1962, *Queensland State Archives*, Box 729 6J/8.

8. Personal communication, Milton Brim, Kuranda, 4 September 1997.

9. Personal communication, Wilfred Levers, Cairns, 24 September 1997.

10. Personal communication, Barry Hunter Snr, 17 July 1997.

11. I. Howie-Willis, 'Referendum 1967', in D. Horton (Gen. Ed.), *The Encyclopaedia of Aboriginal Australia,* Vol. 2, Canberra, 1994, pp. 933–34.

12. Personal communication, Lyn Hobbler, Mantaka, 3 August 1995.

13. Personal communication, Rhonda Brim, Mantaka, 17 August 1995.

14. In 1939 the Act was revised, and again in 1965 (*Aborigines and Torres Strait Islands Affairs Act*), when '[u]nder this Act the Protectorate was abolished and nearly all the provisions relating to people living off reserves repealed. In 1971 the Acts were divided again between aboriginals and islanders and now applied almost entirely to the administration and local government of reserves . . . The reserves councils were gradually given more authority in the running of the reserves but they had neither the personnel nor resources to fulfil their

purpose as local governing bodies'. W. Thaiday, *Under the Act*, N.Q. Black Publishing Co., Townsville, 1981, pp. 6–7. To understand the despicable attitude of the State Government towards Aboriginal people, particularly with regard to deliberately underpaying members of the Aboriginal workforce on communities around Queensland, see R. Kidd, 'Profiting from Poverty: State Policies and Aboriginal Deprivation', *Queensland Review*, UQP, St Lucia, Vol. 4, No. 1, April 1997, pp. 81–86.

15. ' "The Camp" at Redlynch—Can anything be done?', *Northerner*, 7 April 1967, Vol. 67, No. 25.

16. Personal communication, Mr Kelvin Hill, 1990.

17. *Northerner*, 7 April 1967.

18. Personal communication, Mick Miller, 11 November 1997.

19. R. Kidd, *The Way We Civilise*, UQP, St Lucia, p. 270.

20. Personal communication, Mick Miller, 11 November 1997.

21. Endnote 6 in original, p. 370, *Queensland State Archives*, TR254 6C/8, 21.11.69, Hewitt to ministers, ibid., p. 270.

22. R. Kidd, *The Way We Civilise*, p. 271.

23. The current standardised spelling of the Djabugay word meaning 'platypus' is 'Ngunbay'.

24. Personal communication, Rhonda Brim, Mantaka, 16 August 1995.

25. Report attached to letter to Under Sec. from Acting Exec. Officer, Cairns, 27 April 1979, *Queensland State Archives*, 6J/8, File 2.

26. Oral History Interview with Mr Steven Fagan, 31 July 1995.

27. Senator O'Keefe, *The Tablelands Advertiser*, 20 January 1982.

28. In both articles, it is the Queensland Housing Commission and the Department of Community Services officers who 'had co-operated to design the development'; no mention of any consultation or involvement of the Aboriginal people who were to live in this 'entirely new concept in . . . housing . . .', *Cairns Post*, 6 and 8 July 1982.

29. *Cairns Post*, 5 April 1986. See also Lance Riley (Ngoonbi Co-Operative Society) to R. C. Katter, Minister, 23 May 1986, *Queensland State Archives*, Box 729 6J/8, '. . . we are confident of obtaining finance for Six homes at Mantaka during 1986/87. That is, providing ownership of the land is invested in the Society. Over Seventy Aboriginal people are dwelling at Mantaka in One or Two bedroom houses originally located at Mona Mona Mission some Sixty years ago. They are without Septics, Plumbing or Electricity and lterally [sic] falling down from deterioration and lack of maintenance . . .'

30. Personal communication, Rhonda Brim.

31. Personal communication, Martha Brim.

32. This is the spelling of Norman Tindale, which is not as easily pronounced as the current linguistic spelling adopted by the descendants of the Djabugay. For a more precise approach, see R. Banning & M. Quinn, *Djabugay Ngirrma Gulu,* Cairns, 1989, pp. 110–11.

33. 1914–1941 John W. Bleakley, 1941–1963 Cornelius O'Leary, 1964–1986 Patrick Killoran.

34. R. Kidd, *The Way We Civilise*, p. 346.

35. Personal communication, Pastor David Blanch, 15 September 1997.

36. 'The type of history . . . described has created many problems within

Aboriginal communities. One very clear tendency associated with resettlement of people who were "strangers" to the traditional land to which they were moved has been a demonstrable trend for those who are moved into the area of others (recognised in Queensland legislation as "historical people") to become involved in the power structures established by white administrators, far more readily than traditional people, who have always lived there and have simply not felt the need . . . As a result those that became involved controlled the structures when self management became Government policy. Thus employment opportunities tended to go to the historical people rather than the traditional people.' J. Bottoms, 'Clayton's Native Title', Address to Labor Women, as part of the National Reconciliation Process, Brisbane, 12 April 1997, p. 9.

37. Ibid., p. 214.
38. The *Community Services (Aboriginal Lands) Act 1984.*
39. J. Bottoms, 'Clayton's Native Title', Address to Labor Women, as part of the National Reconciliation Process, Brisbane, 12 April 1997, p. 5.
40. *The Australian*, 4 June 1992.
41. Personal communication, Rhonda Duffin, DTAC, Kuranda, 17 August 1995.
42. Ibid.
43. *Cairns Post*, 25 October 1997, p. 1.
44. *Courier Mail*, 2 December 1997.
45. Spokeswoman from the Queensland Department of Natural Resources, Land Section, 3 December 1998.
46. M. Bachelard, *The Great Land Grab*, Hyland House, South Melbourne, 1997, pp. 113–14. This work offers a most comprehensive explanation of the Native Title debate, and the Wik and Mabo judgments of the Australian High Court; essential reading for all Australians.
47. Tim Flannery cogently argues that '[t]he problem of cultural maladaptation seems to be particularly acute in Australia. For it has the highest number of new settlers of any of the 'new' lands, and it has an extremely difficult and unusual ecology. Perhaps this accounts for what outsiders perceive as the obsession Australians have with defining themselves. But to Australians, that obsession makes perfect sense. It arises from a frustration borne of the long-felt inability to live in harmony with the land. It comes from the dismay one feels when seeing the extraordinary beauty and complexity of unique environments wither—even from an apparently gentle touch by a European hand—and from the floods and bushfires that constantly remind Australians that the land does not hold them comfortably. Finally, and most importantly to many, it arises from the great gulf of culture and understanding that exists between Aborigines and other Australians.

As a result of these feelings, Australians have long struggled with the issue of national identity; yet they have done so without really trying to understand the nuts and bolts working of their land. It is now clear I think, that any lasting notion of Australian nationhood must arise from an intimate understanding of Australian ecosystems.' T. Flannery, *The Future Eaters*, Reed Books, Port Melbourne, 1995, pp. 389–90.

Djabugay

Bibliography

OFFICIAL SOURCES

Queensland Votes and Proceedings, 1873–1899.
Queensland Parliamentary Papers, 1900–1963.

SEVENTH DAY ADVENTIST ARCHIVES

The Library, Avondale College, Cooranbong.
Primary Source Material held at Jilli Binna Museum, Kuranda.

QUEENSLAND STATE ARCHIVES

POL 12 M/G1–G2
Mona Mona Mission:
Box Files 729 6J/2–6J/8 (File 1), 6J/9; Box Files 730 6J/10–6J/19; Box Files 731 6J/20–6J/39.
Chief Protector of Aboriginals Office Correspondence, 1913–1941 (6 box files) A/58784, A/69429, A/58861; COL/A139, COL/A306, COL/143M1634.
Chief Protector of Aboriginals Office Correspondence—Home Office Batch Files, 1915–1934, A/5886.
HOM A/34/2473, 03671; TRE/A16 76/1647.

SOUTH AUSTRALIAN MUSEUM

N. B. Tindale Diary Notes on visit to 'Monamona' Mission, August–September, 1938.

NEWSPAPERS

Australasian Record, Cairns Post, Cooktown Courier, Cooktown Herald, Cummins & Campbell Monthly Magazine, Northerner, Port Denison Times, Queenslander, Tablelands Advertiser, Tablelander.

UNPUBLISHED WORKS

Anderson, C. 'The Political and Economic Basis of Kuku-Yalanji Social History', PhD Thesis, University of Queensland, Brisbane, 1984.

Bottoms, J. 'Clayton's Native Title', Address to Labor Women as part of the National Reconciliation Process, Brisbane, 12 April 1997.

Bottoms, T. 'Djarrugan—The Last of the Nesting', M.A. (Qual.) Thesis, James Cook University, Cairns, 1990.

Collins, S. 'Mona Mona: A Culture in Transition', Grad.Dip.Mat.Cult. Thesis, James Cook University, Townsville, 1981.

Cornford, J. 'The Queensland Aboriginals Department 1914–1939', Honours Thesis, James Cook University, Townsville, 1994.

Genever, T. G. 'Black and Blue: Aboriginal–Police Relations in Far North Queensland During the Currency of The Aboriginals Protection and the Restriction of the Sale of Opium Act, 1897–1939', Honours Thesis, James Cook University, Cairns, 1992.

Horsfall, N. 'Living in Rainforest', PhD Thesis, James Cook University, Townsville, 1987.

Kidd, R. 'Regulating Bodies: administrations and Aborigines in Queensland 1840–1988', PhD Thesis, Griffith University, 1994.

Kirkman, N. 'Palmer Gold Fields 1873–1883', Honours Thesis, James Cook University, Townsville, 1984.

PUBLISHED WORKS

All Things Are Connected, TBS Productions Inc. (U.S. TV Documentary), 1994.

Allen, L. & Borey, B. *Cultural and Historical Records of Queensland, Number 2, Annotations to Publications by W. E. Roth*, Anthropology Museum, University of Queensland, St Lucia, 1984.

Alley, G. K. *Riverstone 1877–1977*, *Cairns Post*, Cairns, 1977.

Bachelard, M. *The Great Land Grab*, Hyland House, South Melbourne, 1997.

Banning, R. & Quinn, M. *Djabugay Ngirrma Gulu*, Cairns, 1989.

Banning, R. & Quinn, M. *Bulurru Storywater*, Cairns, 1990.

Black, J. *North Queensland Pioneers*, CWA, Charters Towers, 1931.

Blake, B. J. *Australian Aboriginal Languages*, UQP, St Lucia, 1991.

Bolton, G. C. *A Thousand Miles Away*, ANU, Canberra, 1972.

Boswell, J. *The Life of Samuel Johnson LL.D 1791*, Part One, in *Library of the Future* (Third Edition), World Library, Inc., Irvine, CA., 1993.

Bottoms, T. *The Bama—People of the Rainforest*, Gadja Enterprises, Cairns, 1992.

Bottoms, T. *Yirrganydji Cultural and Historical Trail: A Short Walk On the Wild Side*, Education Queensland, Cairns, 1993.

Broughton, A. D. & Stephens, S. E. *Establishment of Trinity Bay*, Historical Society of Cairns, Cairns, 1984.

Bradley, V. *I didn't know that,* Boolarong Press, Moorooka, 1995.

Breslin, B. *Exterminate With Pride*, James Cook University, Townsville, 1992.

Cairns, J. & Johnston, W. T. *Port Douglas: A History-Sketch Record*, Atherton, 1986.

Canon, W. B. '"Voodoo" Death', *American Anthropology*, Vol. 44, April–June 1942.

Collinson, J. W. 'Genesis of Cairns', Historical Society of Cairns, D1932.

Collinson, J. W. *Early Days of Cairns*, W. R. Smith & Paterson Pty Ltd, Brisbane, 1939.

Connolly, D. M. *Chronicles of Mowbray and Port Douglas,* Cairns, 1984.

David, B. 'Nurrabullgin: Preliminary results from a pre-37,000 year old rockshelter, North Queensland', *Archaeology in Oceania*, 18(1), 1993, pp. 50–54.

Dixon, R. M. W. *The Dyirbal Language of North Queensland*, Cambridge University Press, London, 1972.

Dixon, R. M. W. *A Grammar of Yidiny*, Cambridge University Press, Melbourne, 1977.

Dixon, R. M. W. *Words of Our Country*, UQP, St Lucia, 1991.

Dixon, R. M. W., Ramson, W. S. & Thomas, M. *Aboriginal Words*, Oxford University Press, Melbourne, 1990.

Ellis, R. F. *Rails to the Tableland*, Australian Railway Historical Society, Brisbane, 1985.

Evans, R., Saunders, K. & Cronin, K. *Race Relations in Colonial Queensland: A History of Exclusion, Exploitation and Extermination*, UQP, St Lucia, 1993.

Feetham, J. O. & Rymer, W. V. *North Queensland Jubilee Book 1878–1928*, The Diocese of North Queensland, Townsville, 1929.

Flannery, T. *The Future Eaters*, Reed Books, Port Melbourne, 1995.

Flood, J. *The Riches of Ancient Australia—An Indispensable Guide for Exploring Prehistoric Australia*, UQP, St Lucia, 1990.

Flood, J. *Archaeology of the Dreamtime*, Collins, Sydney, 1989.

Genever, T. G. 'Black and Blue: Aboriginal–Police Relations in Early Far North Queensland', *Historical Society of Cairns*, Bulletin 402, May, 1994.

Gill, J. C. *The Missing Coast—Queensland Takes Shape*, Queensland Museum, South Brisbane, 1988.

Goudberg, N. J., Bonell, M. & Benzaken, D. (Eds), *Tropical Rainforest Research in Australia*, James Cook University, Townsville, May 1990.

Griffin, P. C. *Yarraburra—Myths, Legends and Rock Paintings of the Yarrabah Aboriginal Reserve*, The Humanist Press (Australian Institute of Aboriginal Studies), 1967.

Guginy, Wanyarra & Bina. *Buda:dji Miya Miya Djada*, Cairns, 1991.

Hillier, A. J. 'The Native Police under Scrutiny', *Journal of the Royal Historical Society of Queensland*, Vol. XV, No. 6, February 1994.

129

Horton, D. (Gen. Ed.) *The Encyclopaedia of Aboriginal Australia*, Vols. 1 & 2, Aboriginal Studies Press, Canberra, 1994.

Humston, S. (Ed.) *Kuranda—The Village in the Rainforest 1888–1988*, Brisbane, 1988.

Jones, D. *Trinity Phoenix,* Cairns, 1976.

Johnstone, R. A. *Spinifex and Wattle—Reminiscences of Pioneering in North Queensland,* reprinted, Cairns, 1984.

Kidd, R. 'Profiting from Poverty: State Policies and Aboriginal Deprivation', *Queensland Review*, Vol. 4, No. 1, UQP, St Lucia, April, 1997.

Kidd, R. *The Way We Civilise*, UQP, St Lucia, 1997.

Lack, C. 'The Town That Was Drowned', *Journal of the Royal Historical Society of Queensland*, Vol. 9, No. 2, 1970–71.

Loos, N. *Invasion and Resistance*, ANUP, Canberra, 1982.

Ludlow, P. *The Exiles of Peel Island—Leprosy*, Stones Corner, 1991.

Lumholtz, K. *Among Cannibals*, 1889, ANUP, Canberra, reprinted 1980.

MacLeod, J. & Denoon, D. (Eds), *Health & Healing in Tropical Australia and Papua New Guinea*, James Cook University, Townsville, 1991.

McConnel, U. H. 'The Rainbow-Serpent in North Queensland', *Oceania*, Vol. 1, No. 3, 1930.

McConnel, U. H. 'A Moon Legend From the Bloomfield River, North Queensland', *Oceania*, Vol. 2, No. 1, 1931.

McConnel, U. H. 'Inspiration and Design in Aboriginal Art', *Art in Australia*, 15 May 1935.

McConnel, U. H. 'Mourning Ritual Among the Tribes of Cape York Peninsula', *Oceania*, Vol. 7, No. 3, 1937, pp. 346–73.

McConnel, U. H. 'Social Organization of the Tribes of Cape York Peninsula, North Queensland', *Oceania*, Vol. 10, 1939, pp. 54–72; 1940, pp. 434–55.

McCracken, C. R. 'Some Aboriginal Walking Tracks and Camp Sites in the Douglas Shire, North Queensland', *Queensland Archaeological Research*, Vol. 6, 1989, pp. 103–13.

Meggitt, M. J. *Desert People*, Angus & Robertson, Sydney, 1962.

Mjoberg, E. *Amongst Stone Age People in the Queensland Wilderness*, (1918) translated by S. M. Fryer for the John Oxley Library, Brisbane, 1986.

Petrie, C. *Tom Petrie's Reminiscences of Early Queensland*, 1904, Lloyd O'Niel, Hawthorn, 1975.

Pike, G. *Conquest of the Ranges*, Pinevale Publications, Mareeba, 1984.

Quinn, M. *Djabugay—A Djabugay-English Dictionary*, Queensland Department of Education, Cairns, 1992.

Quinn, M. *Galing Munu-Munu-La*, Mona Mona Aboriginal Corporation, Cairns, 1994.

Quinn, M. *Bama Nganydjin—Our People*, DTAC, Cairns, 1995.

Ramos, A. 'From Eden to limbo: the construction of indigenism in Brazil', pp. 74–88, in G. Clement Bond & A. Gilliam, *Social Construction of the Past—Representation as Power*, Routledge, London, 1994.

Reynolds, H. *The Other Side of the Frontier,* Penguin Books, Ringwood, 1982.

Rivett, D. (Co-Ordinator) *Port Douglas and Environs Planning Study*, Prepared for the Department of the Premier, Economic & Trade Development, Environment Science and Services, Cairns, January 1992.

Rosser, Bill. *Up Rode the Troopers—The Black Police in Queensland*, UQP, St Lucia, 1990.

Roth, W. E. *North Queensland Ethnography,* Vols I–III, Hesperian Press, Victoria Park, reprinted 1984.

Rowan, E. *The Flower Hunter*, Angus & Robertson, North Ryde, 1898.

Savage, P. *Christie Palmerston—Explorer*, James Cook University, Townsville, 1989.

Seaton, D. 'The Initiation Ceremony of the Tjapukai Tribe', *North Queensland Naturalist*, Vol. 26, No. 118, 1 September 1957.

Shapiro, W. *Social Organization in Aboriginal Australia*, ANUP, Canberra, 1979.

Sharp, R. L. 'Ritual Life and Economics of the Yir Yiront of Cape York Peninsula', *Oceania*, Vol. V, 1934, pp. 19–42.

Sharp, R. L. 'Tribes and Totemism in North East Australia', *Oceania*, 1938, Vol. 9, No. 2, pp. 254–75; 1939, Vol. 9, No. 3, pp. 439–61.

Short, E. H. *The Nation Builders*, Watson Ferguson & Co., Brisbane, 1988.

Stanner, W. E. H. 'On Aboriginal Religion', *Oceania*, June 1963, Vol. XXXIII, No. 4, pp. 239–73.

Stanner, W. E. H. 'Aboriginal Organization: Estate, Range, Domain and Regime', *Oceania*, September 1965, Vol. XXXVI, No. 1, pp. 1–26.

Stanner, W. E. H. 'Some Aspects of Aboriginal Religion', *Journal of ANZSTS*, Melbourne, 1976.

Sutherland, J. (Ed.) *Valuing Culture*, Key Issue Paper No. 3, AGPS, Canberra, 1994.

Sutherland, J. (Ed.) *Sharing History*, Key Issue Paper No. 4, AGPS, Canberra, 1994.

Sutton, P. (Ed.) *Languages of Cape York Peninsula*, AIAS, Canberra, 1976.

Swain, T. & Rose, D. B. *Aboriginal Australians and Christian Missions*, AASR, Adelaide, 1988.

Swain, T. *A Place For Strangers: Towards a History of Australian Aboriginal Being*, Cambridge University Press, Melbourne, 1993.

Thaiday, W. *Under the Act*, N.Q. Black Publishing Co., Townsville, 1981.

Thomson, J. (Ed.) *Reaching Back*, Aboriginal Studies Press, Canberra, 1989.

Wills, N. *Give Me Back My Dreaming*, The Communist Art Group, Lota, June 1982.

Winfield, J. G. 'The Hodgkinson Goldfields', *Historical Society of Cairns*, Bulletin 128, March 1970.

Wilmott, W. F. & Stephenson, P. J. *Rocks and Landscapes of the Cairns District*, Queensland Department of Mines, Brisbane, 1989.

ORAL HISTORY

(a) *Interviews with Elders:*

Mrs Enid Boyle, Mrs Jessie Donohue, Mr Lyn Hobbler, Mrs Winnie Brim, Mr Gordon Donohue (d.), Mrs Marita Hobbler, Mr Warren Brim (d.), Mrs Mona Fagan, Mr Selwyn Hunter, Mr Milton Brim, Mr Steven Fagan, Mrs Lorna Mitchell, Mrs Elaine Chookie, Mr Finlay Grogan, Ms Rowena Sheppard, Mrs Esme Hudson, Mrs Florence Williams.

(b) *Interviews with:*

Rhonda Brim, Barry Hunter Snr, Rhonda Duffin, Andy Duffin, Glen Williams, Rosetta Brim, Bill Austen, Mick Miller (d.), Judy Andrews, Martha Brim and Wilton Hobbler.

(c) Published interviews:

Breslin, M. (Co-Ordinator), *Remembering: Interviews of Aboriginal Community Members by Smithfield High Aboriginal Students*, Queensland Education Department, Cairns, 1992.

Cochran, J. 'One House in Malanda: Life Histories of Three Aboriginal Women in Queensland', *Historical Society of Cairns*, 14 May 1993, 305 COC.

Index

Numbers in italics refer to captions to photographs and maps
Numbers in bold type refer to captions to photographs in the colour section after page 98
n = note